53 Low Fat Recipes for Home

By: Kelly Johnson

Table of Contents

- Breakfast:
    - Low-fat yogurt parfait with fresh berries
    - Oatmeal with sliced banana and a drizzle of honey
    - Whole grain toast with avocado and tomato
- Smoothies:
    - Berry Blast Smoothie with skim milk
    - Green Goddess Smoothie with spinach and Greek yogurt
    - Tropical Delight Smoothie with pineapple and coconut water
- Appetizers:
    - Baked sweet potato fries
    - Greek salad skewers with reduced-fat feta
    - Hummus with raw vegetable dippers
- Soups:
    - Minestrone soup with lean protein and whole grains
    - Tomato basil soup with a touch of low-fat cream
    - Lentil soup with vegetables
- Salads:
    - Grilled chicken Caesar salad with a light dressing
    - Quinoa salad with cucumber, cherry tomatoes, and lemon vinaigrette
    - Asian-inspired cabbage salad with a ginger dressing
- Main Dishes - Chicken:
    - Baked lemon herb chicken breasts
    - Grilled chicken with mango salsa

- - Chicken stir-fry with lots of colorful vegetables
- Main Dishes - Fish:
  - Baked salmon with dill and lemon
  - Shrimp and vegetable kebabs
  - Fish tacos with cabbage slaw
- Main Dishes - Vegetarian:
  - Eggplant and zucchini lasagna with low-fat cheese
  - Spinach and mushroom stuffed bell peppers
  - Chickpea and vegetable curry
- Side Dishes:
  - Roasted sweet potato wedges
  - Quinoa pilaf with mixed vegetables
  - Steamed broccoli with a squeeze of lemon
- Pasta:
  - Whole wheat pasta with tomato and basil sauce
  - Zucchini noodles with marinara sauce
  - Shrimp and vegetable pasta with a light garlic sauce
- Grains:
  - Brown rice with black beans and corn
  - Barley and vegetable stir-fry
  - Bulgur wheat salad with herbs and cherry tomatoes
- Desserts:
  - Mixed berry sorbet
  - Angel food cake with fresh strawberries
  - Baked apples with cinnamon and a sprinkle of oats
- Snacks:

- Air-popped popcorn with a dash of nutritional yeast
- Fresh fruit salad
- Greek yogurt with a drizzle of honey

- **Beverages:**
  - Infused water with cucumber and mint
  - Iced green tea with lemon
  - Berry smoothie with low-fat milk or yogurt

- **Grilled Options:**
  - Grilled vegetable skewers
  - Turkey burgers with lean ground turkey
  - Portobello mushroom burgers

- **Crockpot/Slow Cooker Meals:**
  - Chicken and vegetable stew
  - Lentil and vegetable soup
  - Turkey chili with lots of beans and tomatoes

- **Wraps and Roll-ups:**
  - Turkey and avocado wraps with whole wheat tortillas
  - Veggie roll-ups with hummus
  - Smoked salmon pinwheels with low-fat cream cheese

- **Pizza:**
  - Whole wheat pizza with lots of veggies
  - Chicken and vegetable pizza with a thin crust
  - Margherita pizza with a light cheese topping

- **Stir-Fries:**
  - Tofu and broccoli stir-fry
  - Shrimp and snow pea stir-fry

- Chicken and asparagus stir-fry
- Sauces and Dressings:
    - Yogurt-based tzatziki sauce
    - Balsamic vinaigrette with Dijon mustard
    - Salsa verde with fresh herbs

Breakfast:

Low-Fat Yogurt Parfait with Fresh Berries

Ingredients:

- 1 cup low-fat or fat-free vanilla yogurt
- 1/2 cup granola (look for a low-fat or whole grain option)
- 1 cup mixed fresh berries (strawberries, blueberries, raspberries)

Instructions:

Prepare the Yogurt:
- In a bowl, take 1 cup of low-fat or fat-free vanilla yogurt.

Layer the Yogurt:
- Begin by adding a layer of yogurt to the bottom of a glass or a bowl.

Add Granola:
- Sprinkle a layer of granola on top of the yogurt. Granola adds a nice crunch and some healthy whole grains.

Add Berries:
- Add a layer of mixed fresh berries on top of the granola. You can use a combination of strawberries, blueberries, and raspberries for a burst of color and flavor.

Repeat Layers:
- Repeat the layers until you reach the top of the glass or bowl, finishing with a layer of berries on top.

Serve Immediately:

- Enjoy the parfait immediately to maintain the crunchiness of the granola. Alternatively, you can refrigerate it for a short time if you prefer a slightly chilled parfait.

Optional Additions:

- If you want to enhance the flavor, you can drizzle a small amount of honey or maple syrup over the top. Additionally, a sprinkle of chia seeds or sliced almonds can add nutritional value.

This low-fat yogurt parfait is not only delicious but also provides a good balance of protein, fiber, and vitamins from the yogurt and fresh berries. Feel free to customize it with your favorite fruits and toppings!

Oatmeal With Sliced Banana and a Drizzle of Honey

Ingredients:

- 1/2 cup old-fashioned rolled oats
- 1 cup milk (dairy or plant-based)
- 1 ripe banana, sliced
- 1-2 tablespoons honey (adjust to taste)
- Optional toppings: chopped nuts (e.g., almonds or walnuts), a sprinkle of cinnamon

Instructions:

Cook the Oatmeal:

- In a small saucepan, combine the rolled oats and milk. Bring to a simmer over medium heat.

Stir and Simmer:

- Reduce the heat to low and stir the oats frequently. Simmer for about 5-7 minutes or until the oats are cooked and the mixture has thickened to your liking.

Slice the Banana:

- While the oatmeal is cooking, slice the ripe banana into thin rounds.

Assemble the Bowl:

- Once the oatmeal is ready, transfer it to a bowl.

Add Banana Slices:

- Arrange the sliced banana on top of the oatmeal.

Drizzle with Honey:

- Drizzle honey over the oatmeal and banana slices. Adjust the amount of honey based on your sweetness preference.

Optional Toppings:

- If desired, sprinkle chopped nuts (such as almonds or walnuts) over the top for added crunch and nutrition. A dash of cinnamon can also enhance the flavor.

Serve Warm:

- Serve the oatmeal with banana and honey while it's still warm. The heat will help the honey melt and blend into the oats.

Enjoy:

- Mix everything together before each bite to combine the flavors, and enjoy your comforting bowl of oatmeal with the sweetness of banana and honey.

This oatmeal recipe is not only delicious but also provides a good source of fiber, vitamins, and minerals. It's a wholesome and satisfying breakfast option. Feel free to customize it with other fruits or toppings based on your preferences!

Whole Grain Toast with Avocado and Tomato

Ingredients:

- 2 slices of whole grain bread
- 1 ripe avocado
- 1 medium-sized tomato, thinly sliced
- Salt and pepper to taste
- Optional toppings: red pepper flakes, a drizzle of olive oil, fresh cilantro or basil leaves

Instructions:

Toast the Bread:
- Toast the slices of whole grain bread to your preferred level of crispiness.

Prepare the Avocado:
- While the bread is toasting, cut the ripe avocado in half. Remove the pit and scoop the flesh into a bowl.

Mash the Avocado:
- Mash the avocado with a fork until it reaches your desired level of smoothness. You can leave it slightly chunky for texture.

Season the Avocado:
- Add a pinch of salt and pepper to the mashed avocado. Mix well to combine.

Spread Avocado on Toast:
- Once the bread is toasted, spread the mashed avocado evenly over each slice.

Add Tomato Slices:

- Place thinly sliced tomatoes on top of the mashed avocado, covering the entire surface of the toast.

Season Again:

- Sprinkle a bit more salt and pepper over the tomatoes for added flavor.

Optional Toppings:

- If you like, you can add a sprinkle of red pepper flakes for a hint of heat, a drizzle of olive oil for richness, or fresh cilantro or basil leaves for a burst of freshness.

Serve and Enjoy:

- Serve the whole grain toast with avocado and tomato immediately while it's still warm. The combination of creamy avocado and juicy tomato on crunchy whole grain toast is both satisfying and nutritious.

This recipe is a great way to enjoy a quick and wholesome breakfast or snack, packed with healthy fats, fiber, and essential nutrients. Feel free to customize it based on your preferences!

Smoothies:

Berry Blast Smoothie with Skim Milk

Ingredients:

- 1 cup mixed berries (strawberries, blueberries, raspberries)
- 1 banana, peeled and sliced
- 1 cup skim milk
- 1/2 cup plain low-fat yogurt
- 1 tablespoon honey (optional, depending on sweetness preference)
- Ice cubes (optional)

Instructions:

Prepare the Berries:
- If using fresh berries, wash them thoroughly. If using frozen berries, make sure they are unsweetened and ready to use.

Combine Ingredients:
- In a blender, add the mixed berries, sliced banana, skim milk, and plain low-fat yogurt.

Add Honey (Optional):
- If you prefer a sweeter smoothie, add honey to the blender. Adjust the amount based on your sweetness preference.

Blend Until Smooth:

- Blend the ingredients on high speed until you achieve a smooth and creamy consistency. If the smoothie is too thick, you can add more skim milk to reach your desired thickness.

Add Ice Cubes (Optional):

- If you want a colder and icier smoothie, add a handful of ice cubes to the blender and blend until well incorporated.

Taste and Adjust:

- Taste the smoothie and adjust the sweetness or thickness by adding more honey or skim milk if needed.

Pour and Serve:

- Pour the Berry Blast Smoothie into glasses and serve immediately.

Garnish (Optional):

- Optionally, you can garnish the smoothie with a few whole berries on top for a decorative touch.

Enjoy:

- Sip and enjoy this delicious and nutritious Berry Blast Smoothie with Skim Milk!

This smoothie is not only rich in antioxidants from the berries but also provides a good source of vitamins and minerals. It's a perfect way to start your day or to enjoy as a refreshing snack. Feel free to customize the recipe by adding other fruits or adjusting the sweetness to suit your taste preferences.

Green Goddess Smoothie with Spinach and Greek Yogurt

Ingredients:

- 1 cup fresh spinach leaves
- 1/2 cup cucumber, peeled and sliced
- 1/2 avocado, peeled and pitted
- 1/2 cup plain Greek yogurt
- 1/2 banana, peeled
- 1 tablespoon chia seeds (optional)
- 1 cup cold water or coconut water
- Ice cubes (optional)
- Honey or agave syrup for sweetness (optional)

Instructions:

Prepare Ingredients:

- Wash the fresh spinach leaves, peel and slice the cucumber, peel and pit the avocado, and peel the banana.

Combine in Blender:

- In a blender, add the fresh spinach, sliced cucumber, avocado, Greek yogurt, banana, and chia seeds.

Add Liquid:

- Pour in the cold water or coconut water into the blender.

Blend Until Smooth:

- Blend all the ingredients on high speed until the mixture becomes smooth and creamy. If you prefer a colder smoothie, you can add ice cubes to the blender.

Taste and Sweeten (Optional):

- Taste the Green Goddess Smoothie and add honey or agave syrup if you prefer a sweeter flavor. Blend again to combine.

Adjust Consistency:

- If the smoothie is too thick, you can add more water or coconut water until it reaches your desired consistency.

Pour and Serve:

- Pour the Green Goddess Smoothie into glasses and serve immediately.

Garnish (Optional):

- Optionally, you can garnish the smoothie with a slice of cucumber or a sprinkle of chia seeds for a decorative touch.

Enjoy:

- Sip and enjoy this nutrient-packed Green Goddess Smoothie with Spinach and Greek Yogurt!

This smoothie is not only delicious but also rich in vitamins, minerals, and fiber from the spinach and other wholesome ingredients. It's a great way to incorporate greens into your diet and start your day with a burst of energy. Feel free to adjust the ingredients and quantities based on your preferences!

Tropical Delight Smoothie with Pineapple and Coconut Water

Ingredients:

- 1 cup fresh or frozen pineapple chunks
- 1/2 cup mango chunks (fresh or frozen)
- 1/2 banana, peeled
- 1/2 cup coconut water
- 1/2 cup plain or coconut-flavored Greek yogurt
- Ice cubes (optional)
- Honey or agave syrup for sweetness (optional)
- Shredded coconut for garnish (optional)

Instructions:

Prepare Ingredients:
- If using fresh pineapple, peel and cut it into chunks. If using fresh mango, peel and cut it into chunks. Peel the banana.

Combine in Blender:
- In a blender, add the pineapple chunks, mango chunks, peeled banana, coconut water, and Greek yogurt.

Add Ice Cubes (Optional):
- If you prefer a colder smoothie, add a handful of ice cubes to the blender.

Blend Until Smooth:
- Blend all the ingredients on high speed until the mixture becomes smooth and creamy.

Taste and Sweeten (Optional):

- Taste the Tropical Delight Smoothie and add honey or agave syrup if you desire additional sweetness. Blend again to combine.

Adjust Consistency:

- If the smoothie is too thick, you can add more coconut water until it reaches your desired consistency.

Pour and Serve:

- Pour the Tropical Delight Smoothie into glasses.

Garnish (Optional):

- Optionally, you can garnish the smoothie with a sprinkle of shredded coconut for added texture and tropical flair.

Enjoy:

- Sip and enjoy this delightful Tropical Smoothie with the goodness of pineapple and coconut water!

This smoothie is not only delicious but also provides a tropical escape in a glass. It's rich in vitamin C, antioxidants, and hydration from the combination of pineapple and coconut water. Customize the recipe based on your preferences, and feel free to experiment with additional tropical fruits like papaya or kiwi if you like!

Appetizers:

Baked Sweet Potato Fries

Ingredients:

- 2 large sweet potatoes, peeled and cut into fries
- 2 tablespoons olive oil
- 1 teaspoon paprika
- 1/2 teaspoon garlic powder
- 1/2 teaspoon onion powder
- 1/2 teaspoon cayenne pepper (adjust to taste for spiciness)
- Salt and pepper to taste
- Optional: 1 tablespoon cornstarch (for added crispiness)

Instructions:

Preheat the Oven:
- Preheat your oven to 425°F (220°C). Line a baking sheet with parchment paper or lightly grease it.

Prepare the Sweet Potatoes:
- Peel the sweet potatoes and cut them into evenly sized fries. Try to keep them similar in size for even baking.

Soak in Water (Optional):
- If you have time, you can soak the sweet potato fries in cold water for about 30 minutes. This can help remove some of the starch and make them crispier. Pat them dry with a clean kitchen towel before proceeding.

Seasoning Mixture:

- In a bowl, mix together olive oil, paprika, garlic powder, onion powder, cayenne pepper, salt, and pepper. If you want extra crispiness, you can also add cornstarch to the mixture.

Coat the Fries:

- Place the sweet potato fries in a large bowl. Pour the seasoning mixture over the fries and toss until they are evenly coated.

Arrange on Baking Sheet:

- Spread the seasoned sweet potato fries in a single layer on the prepared baking sheet. Make sure they are not overcrowded to allow for even cooking.

Bake in the Oven:

- Bake in the preheated oven for about 20-25 minutes, turning them halfway through the cooking time. Bake until they are golden brown and crispy.

Serve Warm:

- Once the sweet potato fries are done, remove them from the oven. Let them cool for a few minutes before serving.

Enjoy:

- Serve the baked sweet potato fries warm with your favorite dipping sauce. They are great on their own or with options like ketchup, garlic aioli, or sriracha mayo.

This recipe provides a healthier alternative to deep-fried sweet potato fries while still delivering a delicious and satisfying flavor. Adjust the seasonings to your taste preferences and enjoy a tasty side dish or snack!

Greek Salad Skewers with Reduced-Fat Feta

Ingredients:

- Cherry tomatoes
- Cucumber, cut into bite-sized cubes
- Kalamata olives, pitted
- Red onion, cut into small wedges
- Reduced-fat feta cheese, cut into cubes
- Extra virgin olive oil
- Fresh lemon juice
- Dried oregano
- Salt and pepper, to taste
- Wooden or metal skewers

Instructions:

Prepare the Ingredients:
- Wash and cut the cherry tomatoes, cucumber, and red onion into bite-sized pieces.

Assemble the Skewers:
- Thread the cherry tomatoes, cucumber cubes, Kalamata olives, red onion wedges, and reduced-fat feta cheese cubes onto the skewers, alternating the ingredients for a colorful presentation.

Make the Dressing:
- In a small bowl, whisk together extra virgin olive oil, fresh lemon juice, dried oregano, salt, and pepper. Adjust the quantities to taste.

Drizzle the Dressing:
- Drizzle the dressing over the assembled Greek Salad Skewers. You can also brush the skewers with the dressing for an even distribution of flavors.

Serve:
- Arrange the skewers on a serving platter.

Optional Garnish:
- Optionally, sprinkle additional dried oregano over the skewers for a decorative touch.

Chill (Optional):
- If you have time, you can refrigerate the skewers for about 15-30 minutes to allow the flavors to meld.

Serve and Enjoy:
- Serve the Greek Salad Skewers as a refreshing and light appetizer. They are perfect for parties, gatherings, or as a healthy snack.

These Greek Salad Skewers are a delightful way to enjoy the classic flavors of a Greek salad in a convenient and portable form. The reduced-fat feta and the vibrant mix of vegetables make these skewers a healthier option without compromising on taste. Feel free to customize the ingredients and dressing to suit your preferences!

Hummus with Raw Vegetable Dippers

Ingredients:

For Hummus:

- 1 can (15 oz) chickpeas, drained and rinsed (or 1 1/2 cups cooked chickpeas)
- 1/4 cup tahini
- 2 tablespoons extra virgin olive oil
- 2 tablespoons fresh lemon juice
- 1-2 cloves garlic, minced
- 1/2 teaspoon ground cumin
- Salt, to taste
- Water (as needed for desired consistency)

For Raw Vegetable Dippers:

- Carrot sticks
- Celery sticks
- Bell pepper strips (various colors)
- Cucumber slices
- Cherry tomatoes
- Broccoli or cauliflower florets

Instructions:

For Hummus:

    Blend Ingredients:

- In a food processor, combine the chickpeas, tahini, olive oil, lemon juice, minced garlic, ground cumin, and a pinch of salt.

Process Until Smooth:

- Process the ingredients until smooth. If the mixture is too thick, add water, one tablespoon at a time, until you reach your desired consistency.

Adjust Seasoning:

- Taste the hummus and adjust the salt or other seasonings if necessary. You can also add more lemon juice or garlic to suit your taste.

Transfer to a Serving Dish:

- Spoon the hummus into a serving dish. Optionally, create a well in the center and drizzle a bit of extra virgin olive oil over the top.

For Raw Vegetable Dippers:

Prepare Vegetables:

- Wash and cut the carrot, celery, bell pepper, cucumber, cherry tomatoes, and broccoli or cauliflower into bite-sized sticks or slices.

Arrange on a Platter:

- Arrange the prepared raw vegetables on a serving platter.

Serve:

- Serve the hummus alongside the raw vegetable dippers.

Enjoy:

- Dip the raw vegetables into the hummus and enjoy a delicious and nutritious snack!

This recipe provides a colorful and nutrient-packed platter that's perfect for entertaining or as a wholesome snack. The hummus is rich in protein and healthy fats, while the raw vegetables offer a variety of vitamins and crunch. Feel free to customize the vegetables based on your preferences, and enjoy this tasty and healthy combination!

Soups:

Minestrone Soup with Lean Protein and Whole Grains

Ingredients:

- 1 tablespoon olive oil
- 1 onion, diced
- 2 carrots, peeled and diced
- 2 celery stalks, diced
- 3 cloves garlic, minced
- 1 zucchini, diced
- 1 cup green beans, cut into 1-inch pieces
- 1 cup diced tomatoes (fresh or canned)
- 1 can (15 oz) kidney beans, drained and rinsed
- 1 cup cooked whole grain pasta (such as whole wheat or brown rice pasta)
- 8 cups low-sodium vegetable broth
- 1 teaspoon dried oregano
- 1 teaspoon dried basil
- 1/2 teaspoon dried thyme
- Salt and pepper, to taste
- 2 cups fresh spinach or kale, chopped
- 1 cup lean protein (cooked and diced chicken, turkey, or beans)
- Grated Parmesan cheese for serving (optional)

Instructions:

Sauté Aromatics:

- In a large soup pot, heat olive oil over medium heat. Add diced onion, carrots, and celery. Sauté until the vegetables are softened, about 5 minutes.

Add Garlic and Vegetables:

- Add minced garlic and sauté for an additional 1-2 minutes. Then, add diced zucchini, green beans, diced tomatoes, and kidney beans to the pot.

Season:

- Season the vegetables with dried oregano, dried basil, dried thyme, salt, and pepper. Stir well to combine.

Pour in Broth:

- Pour in the low-sodium vegetable broth and bring the soup to a simmer. Let it cook for about 15-20 minutes or until the vegetables are tender.

Add Cooked Pasta and Protein:

- Add the cooked whole grain pasta and your choice of lean protein (chicken, turkey, or beans) to the soup. Stir to combine.

Adjust Seasoning:

- Taste the soup and adjust the seasoning, adding more salt and pepper if needed.

Add Leafy Greens:

- Add the chopped spinach or kale to the soup and let it simmer for an additional 5 minutes until the greens are wilted.

Serve:

- Ladle the Minestrone Soup into bowls. Optionally, sprinkle with grated Parmesan cheese before serving.

Enjoy:

- Serve the soup hot and enjoy a comforting and nutritious bowl of Minestrone with lean protein and whole grains!

This Minestrone Soup is a wholesome and well-balanced meal, providing a mix of vegetables, lean protein, and whole grains. Feel free to customize the recipe by adding your favorite vegetables or adjusting the seasonings according to your taste preferences.

Tomato Basil Soup With a Touch of Low-Fat Cream

Ingredients:

- 2 tablespoons olive oil
- 1 onion, diced
- 3 cloves garlic, minced
- 2 cans (28 oz each) whole tomatoes, undrained
- 1/4 cup tomato paste
- 1 cup vegetable broth (low-sodium)
- 1 teaspoon dried basil
- 1/2 teaspoon dried oregano
- 1/2 teaspoon dried thyme
- Salt and pepper, to taste
- 1/4 cup low-fat or fat-free cream
- Fresh basil leaves for garnish
- Croutons for serving (optional)

Instructions:

Sauté Aromatics:

- In a large pot, heat olive oil over medium heat. Add diced onions and cook until softened, about 5 minutes. Add minced garlic and sauté for an additional 1-2 minutes.

Add Tomatoes:

- Add the whole tomatoes, including the juice, to the pot. Break up the tomatoes with a spoon or spatula. Stir in the tomato paste.

Season:

- Pour in the vegetable broth and add dried basil, dried oregano, dried thyme, salt, and pepper. Stir well to combine.

Simmer:

- Bring the soup to a simmer, then reduce the heat to low. Let it simmer for about 20-25 minutes, allowing the flavors to meld and the soup to thicken.

Blend:

- Using an immersion blender, carefully blend the soup until smooth. Alternatively, transfer the soup to a blender in batches, blending until smooth, and return it to the pot.

Add Cream:

- Stir in the low-fat or fat-free cream, and let the soup simmer for an additional 5 minutes.

Adjust Seasoning:

- Taste the soup and adjust the seasoning, adding more salt and pepper if needed.

Serve:

- Ladle the Tomato Basil Soup into bowls. Garnish with fresh basil leaves and croutons if desired.

Enjoy:

- Serve the soup hot and enjoy the comforting flavors of tomato and basil with a touch of low-fat cream!

This Tomato Basil Soup is creamy and flavorful with the addition of low-fat cream. It's a comforting and classic soup that pairs well with a side of crusty bread or a simple salad. Adjust the cream quantity based on your preference for richness.

Salads:

Lentil Soup with Vegetables

Ingredients:

- 1 cup dried green or brown lentils, rinsed and drained
- 2 tablespoons olive oil
- 1 onion, diced
- 2 carrots, peeled and diced
- 2 celery stalks, diced
- 3 cloves garlic, minced
- 1 teaspoon ground cumin
- 1 teaspoon ground coriander
- 1/2 teaspoon smoked paprika
- 1/2 teaspoon turmeric
- 1 bay leaf
- 1 can (14 oz) diced tomatoes
- 6 cups vegetable broth (low-sodium)
- Salt and pepper, to taste
- 2 cups chopped spinach or kale
- Juice of 1 lemon
- Fresh parsley for garnish

Instructions:

    Prepare Lentils:

- Rinse the lentils under cold water and set them aside.

Sauté Vegetables:

- In a large pot, heat olive oil over medium heat. Add diced onion, carrots, and celery. Sauté until the vegetables are softened, about 5 minutes.

Add Garlic and Spices:

- Add minced garlic, ground cumin, ground coriander, smoked paprika, turmeric, and the bay leaf. Stir well to coat the vegetables with the spices.

Add Lentils and Tomatoes:

- Add the rinsed lentils, diced tomatoes (with their juices), and vegetable broth to the pot. Stir to combine.

Simmer:

- Bring the soup to a boil, then reduce the heat to low, cover, and let it simmer for about 25-30 minutes or until the lentils are tender.

Season:

- Season the soup with salt and pepper to taste. Adjust the seasoning as needed.

Add Leafy Greens:

- Stir in the chopped spinach or kale and let it simmer for an additional 5 minutes until the greens are wilted.

Finish with Lemon Juice:

- Squeeze the juice of one lemon into the soup and stir to combine. Adjust the lemon juice according to your taste preferences.

Serve:

- Ladle the Lentil Soup into bowls. Garnish with fresh parsley.

Enjoy:

- Serve the soup hot and enjoy this nutritious and flavorful Lentil Soup with Vegetables!

This lentil soup is not only delicious but also packed with protein, fiber, and a variety of vitamins and minerals. It's a comforting and satisfying meal, perfect for cooler days. Feel free to customize the recipe by adding your favorite vegetables or adjusting the spices to suit your taste.

Grilled Chicken Caesar Salad With a Light Dressing

Ingredients:

For the Grilled Chicken:

- 2 boneless, skinless chicken breasts
- 2 tablespoons olive oil
- 1 teaspoon garlic powder
- Salt and black pepper, to taste
- 1 lemon, juiced

For the Caesar Salad:

- Romaine lettuce, washed and chopped
- Cherry tomatoes, halved
- Croutons (store-bought or homemade)
- Shaved Parmesan cheese

For the Light Caesar Dressing:

- 1/3 cup plain Greek yogurt
- 2 tablespoons grated Parmesan cheese
- 1 tablespoon Dijon mustard
- 1 tablespoon lemon juice
- 1 teaspoon Worcestershire sauce
- 1 clove garlic, minced
- Salt and black pepper, to taste

- 2 tablespoons olive oil

Instructions:

Grilled Chicken:

   Preheat the grill or grill pan over medium-high heat.

   In a bowl, mix together olive oil, garlic powder, salt, pepper, and lemon juice to create a marinade.

   Coat the chicken breasts with the marinade on both sides.

   Grill the chicken for about 6-8 minutes per side or until fully cooked (internal temperature reaches 165°F or 74°C).

   Once cooked, let the chicken rest for a few minutes before slicing it into thin strips.

Caesar Salad:

   In a large salad bowl, combine the chopped Romaine lettuce, cherry tomatoes, croutons, and shaved Parmesan cheese.

Light Caesar Dressing:

   In a small bowl, whisk together Greek yogurt, grated Parmesan cheese, Dijon mustard, lemon juice, Worcestershire sauce, minced garlic, salt, and pepper. Gradually whisk in olive oil until the dressing is smooth and well combined.

Assembling the Salad:

   Add the grilled chicken strips to the salad.

Drizzle the light Caesar dressing over the salad and toss until everything is well coated.

Serve immediately, and if desired, garnish with additional Parmesan cheese and croutons.

Enjoy your Grilled Chicken Caesar Salad with a light and flavorful dressing!

This recipe provides a healthier take on the classic Caesar salad by using a light dressing made with Greek yogurt. It's a delicious and satisfying meal that can be enjoyed for lunch or dinner. Adjust the quantities according to your preferences and dietary needs.

Quinoa Salad with Cucumber, Cherry Tomatoes, and Lemon Vinaigrette

Ingredients:

For the Quinoa Salad:

- 1 cup quinoa, rinsed
- 2 cups water or vegetable broth
- 1 cucumber, diced
- 1 cup cherry tomatoes, halved
- 1/4 cup red onion, finely chopped
- 1/4 cup fresh parsley, chopped
- 1/4 cup feta cheese, crumbled (optional)
- Salt and black pepper, to taste

For the Lemon Vinaigrette:

- 1/4 cup extra virgin olive oil
- 2 tablespoons fresh lemon juice
- 1 teaspoon Dijon mustard
- 1 clove garlic, minced
- 1 teaspoon honey or maple syrup
- Salt and black pepper, to taste

Instructions:

For the Quinoa:

In a medium saucepan, combine quinoa and water or vegetable broth. Bring to a boil, then reduce heat to low, cover, and simmer for 15-20 minutes or until the quinoa is cooked and water is absorbed.

Fluff the quinoa with a fork and let it cool to room temperature.

For the Lemon Vinaigrette:

In a small bowl, whisk together olive oil, fresh lemon juice, Dijon mustard, minced garlic, honey or maple syrup, salt, and black pepper. Set aside.

Assembling the Quinoa Salad:

In a large bowl, combine the cooked and cooled quinoa, diced cucumber, cherry tomatoes, chopped red onion, and fresh parsley.

If using feta cheese, add it to the salad.

Pour the lemon vinaigrette over the salad and toss gently to combine, ensuring all ingredients are well coated.

Season with salt and black pepper to taste.

Refrigerate the quinoa salad for at least 30 minutes to allow the flavors to meld.

Before serving, give the salad a final toss and adjust the seasoning if needed.

Serve chilled and enjoy your Quinoa Salad with Cucumber, Cherry Tomatoes, and Lemon Vinaigrette!

This quinoa salad is not only vibrant and flavorful but also a great source of protein, fiber, and essential nutrients. It's perfect as a light lunch or a side dish for dinner. Feel free to customize the recipe by adding other vegetables or herbs according to your taste preferences.

Asian-Inspired Cabbage Salad with a Ginger Dressing

Ingredients:

For the Salad:

- 4 cups shredded green cabbage
- 2 cups shredded red cabbage
- 1 large carrot, julienned or grated
- 1 red bell pepper, thinly sliced
- 1 cup edamame (steamed and cooled)
- 1/4 cup chopped green onions
- 1/4 cup chopped cilantro
- 1/4 cup chopped peanuts or cashews (optional, for garnish)
- Sesame seeds for garnish (optional)

For the Ginger Dressing:

- 3 tablespoons soy sauce (low-sodium)
- 2 tablespoons rice vinegar
- 1 tablespoon sesame oil
- 1 tablespoon fresh ginger, grated
- 1 tablespoon honey or maple syrup
- 1 clove garlic, minced
- 2 tablespoons vegetable oil (such as canola or grapeseed oil)
- Salt and black pepper, to taste

Instructions:

For the Salad:

In a large bowl, combine the shredded green cabbage, shredded red cabbage, julienned carrot, sliced red bell pepper, edamame, chopped green onions, and chopped cilantro.

Toss the salad ingredients together until well mixed.

If using, sprinkle chopped peanuts or cashews and sesame seeds over the top for garnish.

For the Ginger Dressing:

In a small bowl, whisk together soy sauce, rice vinegar, sesame oil, grated fresh ginger, honey or maple syrup, minced garlic, vegetable oil, salt, and black pepper until well combined.

Adjust the sweetness or saltiness to your taste preference.

Assembling the Salad:

Drizzle the ginger dressing over the salad.

Toss the salad gently until all the ingredients are coated with the dressing.

Allow the salad to sit for a few minutes before serving to let the flavors meld.

Serve chilled, and garnish with additional chopped peanuts or cashews and sesame seeds if desired.

Enjoy your refreshing and flavorful Asian-inspired Cabbage Salad with Ginger Dressing!

This salad is not only vibrant and delicious but also packed with crunchy textures and a zesty ginger flavor. It makes a perfect side dish or a light meal on its own. Feel free to customize the ingredients or add protein like grilled chicken or tofu for a heartier option.

Main Dishes - Chicken:

Baked Lemon Herb Chicken Breasts

Ingredients:

- 4 boneless, skinless chicken breasts
- 2 tablespoons olive oil
- 2 tablespoons fresh lemon juice
- 2 teaspoons dried thyme
- 1 teaspoon dried rosemary
- 1 teaspoon dried oregano
- 1 teaspoon garlic powder
- 1 teaspoon onion powder
- Salt and black pepper, to taste
- Lemon slices for garnish (optional)
- Fresh parsley for garnish (optional)

Instructions:

Preheat the Oven:
- Preheat your oven to 400°F (200°C).

Prepare the Chicken Breasts:
- Pat the chicken breasts dry with paper towels. This helps the seasoning adhere better.

Season the Chicken:

- In a small bowl, mix together olive oil, fresh lemon juice, dried thyme, dried rosemary, dried oregano, garlic powder, onion powder, salt, and black pepper to create a marinade.

Marinate the Chicken:

- Place the chicken breasts in a shallow dish or a zip-top plastic bag. Pour the marinade over the chicken, making sure each breast is well coated. You can marinate for at least 15-30 minutes for more flavor, or you can proceed immediately.

Bake the Chicken:

- Place the marinated chicken breasts in a baking dish. Bake in the preheated oven for about 20-25 minutes or until the internal temperature reaches 165°F (74°C) and the chicken is cooked through.

Optional Broiling (for color):

- If you want additional color on the chicken, you can broil for an additional 2-3 minutes, watching closely to avoid burning.

Garnish and Serve:

- Once done, remove the chicken from the oven. Garnish with lemon slices and fresh parsley if desired.

Rest and Slice:

- Let the chicken rest for a few minutes before slicing. This allows the juices to redistribute and keeps the chicken moist.

Serve:

- Serve the Baked Lemon Herb Chicken Breasts with your favorite sides, such as roasted vegetables, quinoa, or a fresh salad.

Enjoy:

- Enjoy your flavorful and tender Baked Lemon Herb Chicken!

This recipe results in juicy and aromatic chicken with a perfect balance of lemon and herbs. It's a versatile dish that pairs well with a variety of sides, making it a great option for a simple and delicious meal.

Grilled Chicken with Mango Salsa

Ingredients:

For the Grilled Chicken:

- 4 boneless, skinless chicken breasts
- 2 tablespoons olive oil
- 1 teaspoon ground cumin
- 1 teaspoon smoked paprika
- 1 teaspoon garlic powder
- Salt and black pepper, to taste
- Lime wedges for serving

For the Mango Salsa:

- 2 ripe mangoes, peeled, pitted, and diced
- 1/2 red onion, finely chopped
- 1 red bell pepper, diced
- 1 jalapeño, seeds removed and finely chopped (optional for heat)
- 1/4 cup fresh cilantro, chopped
- Juice of 1 lime
- Salt and black pepper, to taste

Instructions:

For the Grilled Chicken:

    Preheat the Grill:

- Preheat your grill to medium-high heat.

Season the Chicken:

- In a small bowl, mix together olive oil, ground cumin, smoked paprika, garlic powder, salt, and black pepper to create a marinade.

Marinate the Chicken:

- Brush the chicken breasts with the marinade, making sure to coat both sides.

Grill the Chicken:

- Grill the chicken breasts for approximately 6-8 minutes per side or until the internal temperature reaches 165°F (74°C) and the chicken is cooked through.

Let it Rest:

- Remove the chicken from the grill and let it rest for a few minutes before serving.

Serve:

- Serve the grilled chicken with lime wedges on the side.

For the Mango Salsa:

Prepare the Mango Salsa:

- In a bowl, combine diced mangoes, chopped red onion, diced red bell pepper, chopped jalapeño (if using), chopped cilantro, and lime juice.

Season the Salsa:

- Season the salsa with salt and black pepper to taste. Toss gently to combine.

Chill (Optional):

- If time allows, let the mango salsa chill in the refrigerator for 15-30 minutes to allow the flavors to meld.

Assembly:

Serve Together:
- Spoon the mango salsa over the grilled chicken breasts.

Garnish (Optional):
- Garnish with additional cilantro if desired.

Enjoy:
- Enjoy your Grilled Chicken with Mango Salsa!

This recipe combines the smoky flavors of grilled chicken with the sweet and tangy freshness of mango salsa, creating a delicious and vibrant dish. It's perfect for a light and flavorful summer meal. Adjust the spice level in the salsa according to your preference.

Chicken Stir-Fry with Lots of Colorful Vegetables

Ingredients:

For the Chicken Marinade:

- 1 lb (450g) boneless, skinless chicken breasts, thinly sliced
- 2 tablespoons soy sauce (low-sodium)
- 1 tablespoon oyster sauce
- 1 tablespoon cornstarch
- 1 teaspoon sesame oil
- 1 teaspoon grated ginger
- 2 cloves garlic, minced
- Black pepper, to taste

For the Stir-Fry:

- 2 tablespoons vegetable oil
- 1 bell pepper, thinly sliced (any color)
- 1 carrot, julienned or thinly sliced
- 1 cup broccoli florets
- 1 cup snap peas, ends trimmed
- 1 cup baby corn, halved
- 1 cup mushrooms, sliced
- 3 green onions, sliced (white and green parts separated)
- 2 tablespoons soy sauce (low-sodium)
- 1 tablespoon oyster sauce
- 1 tablespoon hoisin sauce
- 1 teaspoon sesame oil
- 1 teaspoon cornstarch mixed with 2 tablespoons water (optional, for thickening)

Instructions:

1. Marinate the Chicken:

- In a bowl, combine the thinly sliced chicken with soy sauce, oyster sauce, cornstarch, sesame oil, grated ginger, minced garlic, and black pepper. Let it marinate for at least 15-20 minutes.

2. Stir-Fry:

Heat 1 tablespoon of vegetable oil in a wok or large skillet over high heat.
Add the marinated chicken and stir-fry for 2-3 minutes or until it's cooked through. Remove the chicken from the wok and set it aside.
In the same wok, add another tablespoon of vegetable oil.
Add the sliced bell pepper, julienned carrot, broccoli florets, snap peas, baby corn, mushrooms, and the white parts of the green onions. Stir-fry for 3-4 minutes or until the vegetables are crisp-tender.
Return the cooked chicken to the wok with the vegetables.
In a small bowl, mix together soy sauce, oyster sauce, hoisin sauce, and sesame oil. Pour the sauce over the chicken and vegetables.
Toss everything together until well coated and heated through.
If you prefer a thicker sauce, add the cornstarch-water mixture and stir until the sauce thickens.
Stir in the green parts of the sliced green onions.

3. Serve:

- Serve the chicken stir-fry over rice or noodles.

4. Enjoy:

- Enjoy your colorful and flavorful Chicken Stir-Fry with lots of vegetables!

Feel free to customize the vegetables based on your preferences or what you have on hand. This stir-fry is not only delicious but also a quick and healthy meal option. Adjust the level of spiciness or sweetness in the sauce to suit your taste.

Main Dishes - Fish:

Baked Salmon with Dill and Lemon

Ingredients:

- 4 salmon fillets (about 6 ounces each)
- 2 tablespoons olive oil
- Salt and black pepper, to taste
- 2 tablespoons fresh dill, chopped
- Zest of 1 lemon
- Juice of 1 lemon
- Lemon slices for garnish (optional)

Instructions:

Preheat the Oven:
- Preheat your oven to 400°F (200°C).

Prepare the Salmon:
- Place the salmon fillets on a parchment-lined or lightly greased baking sheet.

Season the Salmon:
- Drizzle olive oil over the salmon fillets, ensuring they are well-coated. Sprinkle salt and black pepper to taste.

Add Dill and Lemon Zest:
- Sprinkle the chopped fresh dill over the salmon fillets. Grate the zest of one lemon over the top.

Lemon Juice:

- Squeeze the juice of one lemon over the salmon fillets.

Bake in the Oven:

- Bake the salmon in the preheated oven for about 12-15 minutes or until the salmon is cooked through and flakes easily with a fork.

Garnish (Optional):

- Garnish with additional lemon slices if desired.

Serve:

- Serve the Baked Salmon with Dill and Lemon hot.

Enjoy:

- Enjoy your flavorful and healthy baked salmon!

This recipe is quick and easy, allowing the natural flavors of the salmon to shine with the brightness of dill and lemon. It's a perfect dish for a light and nutritious meal. Pair it with your favorite side dishes, such as steamed vegetables, quinoa, or a fresh salad.

Asian-Inspired Cabbage Salad with a Ginger Dressing

Ingredients:

For the Salad:

- 4 cups shredded green cabbage
- 2 cups shredded red cabbage
- 1 large carrot, julienned or grated
- 1 bell pepper (any color), thinly sliced
- 1 cup edamame, cooked and cooled
- 1/4 cup chopped fresh cilantro
- 1/4 cup sliced green onions
- 1/4 cup chopped peanuts or almonds (optional, for garnish)
- Sesame seeds for garnish (optional)

For the Ginger Dressing:

- 3 tablespoons soy sauce (low-sodium)
- 2 tablespoons rice vinegar
- 1 tablespoon sesame oil
- 1 tablespoon fresh ginger, grated
- 1 tablespoon honey or maple syrup
- 1 clove garlic, minced
- 1/4 cup neutral oil (such as vegetable or canola oil)
- Salt and black pepper, to taste

Instructions:

For the Salad:

In a large bowl, combine shredded green cabbage, shredded red cabbage, julienned carrot, sliced bell pepper, edamame, chopped cilantro, and sliced green onions.

Toss the salad ingredients together until well mixed.

If using, sprinkle chopped peanuts or almonds and sesame seeds over the top for garnish.

For the Ginger Dressing:

In a small bowl, whisk together soy sauce, rice vinegar, sesame oil, grated fresh ginger, honey or maple syrup, minced garlic, salt, and black pepper.

Gradually whisk in neutral oil until the dressing is well combined.

Assembling the Salad:

Drizzle the ginger dressing over the salad.

Toss the salad gently until all the ingredients are coated with the dressing.

Allow the salad to sit for a few minutes before serving to let the flavors meld.

Serve chilled, and garnish with additional chopped peanuts or almonds and sesame seeds if desired.

Enjoy your Asian-inspired Cabbage Salad with Ginger Dressing!

This salad is not only vibrant and flavorful but also a great source of crunch and freshness. The ginger dressing adds a zesty and aromatic touch to the vegetables. It's perfect as a side dish or a light, refreshing meal on its own. Adjust the ingredients or dressing quantities based on your preferences.

Baked Salmon with Dill and Lemon

Ingredients:

- 4 salmon fillets (about 6 ounces each)
- 2 tablespoons olive oil
- Salt and black pepper, to taste
- 2 tablespoons fresh dill, chopped
- Zest of 1 lemon
- Juice of 1 lemon
- Lemon slices for garnish (optional)

Instructions:

Preheat the Oven:
- Preheat your oven to 400°F (200°C).

Prepare the Salmon:
- Place the salmon fillets on a parchment-lined or lightly greased baking sheet.

Season the Salmon:
- Drizzle olive oil over the salmon fillets, ensuring they are well-coated. Sprinkle salt and black pepper to taste.

Add Dill and Lemon Zest:
- Sprinkle the chopped fresh dill over the salmon fillets. Grate the zest of one lemon over the top.

Lemon Juice:
- Squeeze the juice of one lemon over the salmon fillets.

Bake in the Oven:
- Bake the salmon in the preheated oven for about 12-15 minutes or until the salmon is cooked through and flakes easily with a fork.

Garnish (Optional):
- Garnish with additional lemon slices if desired.

Serve:
- Serve the Baked Salmon with Dill and Lemon hot.

Enjoy:
- Enjoy your flavorful and healthy baked salmon!

This recipe is quick and easy, allowing the natural flavors of the salmon to shine with the brightness of dill and lemon. It's a perfect dish for a light and nutritious meal. Pair it with your favorite side dishes, such as steamed vegetables, quinoa, or a fresh salad.

Shrimp and Vegetable Kebabs

Ingredients:

For the Marinade:

- 1/4 cup olive oil
- 2 tablespoons soy sauce (low-sodium)
- 1 tablespoon honey
- 2 cloves garlic, minced
- 1 teaspoon grated fresh ginger
- 1 teaspoon lemon zest
- 1 tablespoon lemon juice
- 1 teaspoon paprika
- Salt and black pepper, to taste

For the Shrimp and Vegetable Kebabs:

- 1 pound large shrimp, peeled and deveined
- 1 bell pepper (any color), cut into chunks
- 1 red onion, cut into chunks
- 1 zucchini, sliced into rounds
- Cherry tomatoes
- Wooden or metal skewers (if using wooden skewers, soak them in water for about 30 minutes)

Instructions:

1. Prepare the Marinade:

- In a bowl, whisk together olive oil, soy sauce, honey, minced garlic, grated ginger, lemon zest, lemon juice, paprika, salt, and black pepper.

2. Marinate the Shrimp:

- Place the peeled and deveined shrimp in a zip-top bag or shallow dish. Pour half of the marinade over the shrimp, making sure they are well-coated. Reserve the other half of the marinade for later.
- Let the shrimp marinate in the refrigerator for at least 30 minutes to allow the flavors to meld.

3. Assemble the Kebabs:

- Preheat your grill or grill pan to medium-high heat.
- Thread the marinated shrimp, bell pepper chunks, red onion chunks, zucchini rounds, and cherry tomatoes onto the skewers, alternating between shrimp and vegetables.

4. Grill the Kebabs:

- Brush the kebabs with the reserved marinade.
- Grill the kebabs for about 2-3 minutes per side, or until the shrimp are opaque and the vegetables are tender.

5. Serve:

- Remove the kebabs from the grill and serve immediately.

6. Enjoy:

- Enjoy your delicious Shrimp and Vegetable Kebabs! They pair well with rice, quinoa, or a fresh salad.

Feel free to customize the vegetables or adjust the seasonings according to your taste preferences. This recipe is perfect for a quick and flavorful meal, especially during outdoor grilling season.

Fish Tacos with Cabbage Slaw

Ingredients:

For the Fish Tacos:

- 1 lb white fish fillets (such as tilapia or cod)
- 1 tablespoon olive oil
- 1 teaspoon ground cumin
- 1 teaspoon chili powder
- 1/2 teaspoon garlic powder
- 1/2 teaspoon smoked paprika
- Salt and black pepper, to taste
- Corn or flour tortillas (small size)
- Lime wedges for serving

For the Cabbage Slaw:

- 2 cups shredded green cabbage
- 1 cup shredded purple cabbage
- 1 carrot, julienned or grated
- 1/4 cup chopped fresh cilantro
- 2 tablespoons mayonnaise
- 2 tablespoons Greek yogurt or sour cream
- 1 tablespoon apple cider vinegar
- 1 tablespoon honey
- Salt and black pepper, to taste

Optional Toppings:

- Sliced avocado
- Salsa or pico de gallo
- Jalapeño slices

Instructions:

For the Fish Tacos:

    Prepare the Fish:

- Pat the fish fillets dry with paper towels. In a small bowl, mix together olive oil, ground cumin, chili powder, garlic powder, smoked paprika, salt, and black pepper.

Marinate the Fish:
- Brush the fish fillets with the spice mixture, ensuring they are well-coated. Let them marinate for about 15-30 minutes.

Cook the Fish:
- Heat a skillet or grill pan over medium-high heat. Cook the fish fillets for 2-3 minutes per side or until they are opaque and flake easily with a fork.

Warm the Tortillas:
- In the same skillet, warm the tortillas for about 20-30 seconds on each side.

For the Cabbage Slaw:

Prepare the Slaw:
- In a large bowl, combine shredded green cabbage, shredded purple cabbage, julienned carrot, and chopped cilantro.

Make the Dressing:
- In a small bowl, whisk together mayonnaise, Greek yogurt (or sour cream), apple cider vinegar, honey, salt, and black pepper.

Combine and Toss:
- Pour the dressing over the cabbage mixture and toss until everything is well-coated.

Assembly:

Assemble the Tacos:
- Place a spoonful of the cabbage slaw on each tortilla.

Add the Fish:
- Top the slaw with a piece of cooked fish.

Optional Toppings:
- Garnish with sliced avocado, salsa or pico de gallo, and jalapeño slices.

Serve:
- Serve the fish tacos with lime wedges on the side.

Enjoy:
- Enjoy your delicious Fish Tacos with Cabbage Slaw!

These fish tacos are not only flavorful but also versatile. Feel free to customize them with your favorite toppings and adjust the spice level to your liking. They make for a perfect light and refreshing meal.

Main Dishes - Vegetarian:

Eggplant and Zucchini Lasagna with Low-Fat Cheese

Ingredients:

For the Vegetable Layers:

- 1 large eggplant, thinly sliced
- 2 medium zucchinis, thinly sliced
- Salt, for sweating the eggplant
- Olive oil, for brushing the vegetables

For the Tomato Sauce:

- 2 tablespoons olive oil
- 1 onion, finely chopped
- 3 cloves garlic, minced
- 1 can (28 oz) crushed tomatoes
- 1 teaspoon dried oregano
- 1 teaspoon dried basil
- Salt and black pepper, to taste

For the Low-Fat Cheese Filling:

- 1 1/2 cups low-fat ricotta cheese
- 1 cup low-fat mozzarella cheese, shredded
- 1/2 cup grated Parmesan cheese
- 1 egg
- 2 tablespoons fresh basil, chopped
- Salt and black pepper, to taste

Additional Layers:

- 9 lasagna noodles, cooked according to package instructions

Instructions:

1. Prepare the Vegetables:

- Sprinkle the eggplant slices with salt and let them sit for about 15-20 minutes. This helps draw out excess moisture. Pat the eggplant slices dry with paper towels.
- Preheat the oven to 375°F (190°C).
- Brush the eggplant and zucchini slices with olive oil and roast them in the oven for about 15-20 minutes or until they are softened. Set aside.

2. Prepare the Tomato Sauce:

   In a saucepan, heat olive oil over medium heat. Add chopped onions and cook until they are softened.
   Add minced garlic and cook for an additional 1-2 minutes until fragrant.
   Pour in the crushed tomatoes and add dried oregano, dried basil, salt, and black pepper. Simmer the sauce for about 15-20 minutes, stirring occasionally. Adjust the seasoning to taste.

3. Prepare the Low-Fat Cheese Filling:

   In a bowl, combine low-fat ricotta cheese, shredded low-fat mozzarella cheese, grated Parmesan cheese, egg, chopped fresh basil, salt, and black pepper. Mix until well combined.

4. Assemble the Lasagna:

   In a baking dish, spread a thin layer of tomato sauce on the bottom.
   Place three cooked lasagna noodles side by side.
   Layer half of the roasted eggplant and zucchini slices over the noodles.
   Spread half of the low-fat cheese filling over the vegetables.
   Repeat the layers: noodles, remaining vegetables, and remaining cheese filling.
   Top with the remaining three lasagna noodles and cover them with the remaining tomato sauce.

5. Bake:

   Cover the baking dish with aluminum foil and bake in the preheated oven for about 30-35 minutes.
   Remove the foil and bake for an additional 10-15 minutes or until the lasagna is hot and bubbly, and the top is lightly browned.

6. Let it Rest:

- Let the lasagna rest for about 10 minutes before slicing and serving.

7. Enjoy:

- Serve the Eggplant and Zucchini Lasagna with Low-Fat Cheese, and enjoy a healthier take on this classic dish!

Feel free to customize the recipe with your favorite herbs, spices, or additional vegetables. This version offers a lighter alternative with low-fat cheese and plenty of flavorful vegetables.

Spinach and Mushroom Stuffed Bell Peppers

Ingredients:

- 4 large bell peppers (any color), halved and seeds removed
- 1 tablespoon olive oil
- 1 onion, finely chopped
- 2 cloves garlic, minced
- 8 oz (about 225g) mushrooms, finely chopped
- 2 cups fresh spinach, chopped
- 1 cup cooked quinoa or rice
- 1 cup shredded mozzarella cheese (or your choice of cheese)
- 1/2 cup grated Parmesan cheese
- 1 teaspoon dried oregano
- 1 teaspoon dried thyme
- Salt and black pepper, to taste
- 1 can (14 oz) diced tomatoes, drained
- Fresh parsley, chopped, for garnish (optional)

Instructions:

Preheat the Oven:
- Preheat your oven to 375°F (190°C).

Prepare the Bell Peppers:
- Cut the bell peppers in half lengthwise, remove the seeds, and place them in a baking dish.

Saute the Vegetables:
- In a large skillet, heat olive oil over medium heat. Add chopped onions and cook until softened.
- Add minced garlic and cook for an additional 1-2 minutes until fragrant.
- Stir in chopped mushrooms and cook until they release their moisture and become golden brown.
- Add chopped spinach to the skillet and cook until wilted. Season with salt and black pepper to taste.

Combine Ingredients:
- In a large bowl, combine the cooked mushroom and spinach mixture with cooked quinoa or rice, shredded mozzarella cheese, grated Parmesan cheese, dried oregano, dried thyme, and drained diced tomatoes. Mix well.

Stuff the Bell Peppers:

- Stuff each bell pepper half with the spinach and mushroom mixture, pressing the filling down slightly.

Bake in the Oven:
- Cover the baking dish with aluminum foil and bake in the preheated oven for about 25-30 minutes or until the peppers are tender.
- Remove the foil and bake for an additional 5-10 minutes until the cheese on top is melted and bubbly.

Garnish and Serve:
- Remove the stuffed bell peppers from the oven. Garnish with chopped fresh parsley if desired.

Enjoy:
- Serve the Spinach and Mushroom Stuffed Bell Peppers hot and enjoy this delicious and nutritious meal!

Feel free to customize the stuffing by adding your favorite herbs, spices, or additional vegetables. These stuffed bell peppers are a great option for a wholesome and vegetarian-friendly meal.

Chickpea and Vegetable Curry

Ingredients:

- 1 tablespoon vegetable oil
- 1 onion, finely chopped
- 3 cloves garlic, minced
- 1 tablespoon ginger, grated
- 1 bell pepper, diced
- 2 carrots, sliced
- 1 zucchini, diced
- 1 can (15 oz) chickpeas, drained and rinsed
- 1 can (14 oz) diced tomatoes
- 1 can (13.5 oz) coconut milk (full-fat or light)
- 2 tablespoons curry powder
- 1 teaspoon ground cumin
- 1 teaspoon ground coriander
- 1/2 teaspoon turmeric
- 1/2 teaspoon cayenne pepper (adjust to taste for spice level)
- Salt and black pepper, to taste
- Fresh cilantro, chopped, for garnish
- Cooked rice or naan, for serving

Instructions:

Saute the Aromatics:
- In a large skillet or pot, heat vegetable oil over medium heat. Add chopped onion and sauté until softened.
- Add minced garlic and grated ginger, and sauté for an additional 1-2 minutes until fragrant.

Add Vegetables:
- Add diced bell pepper, sliced carrots, and diced zucchini to the skillet. Cook for about 5 minutes until the vegetables start to soften.

Add Chickpeas and Tomatoes:
- Add drained and rinsed chickpeas and diced tomatoes (with their juice) to the skillet. Stir well to combine.

Prepare the Curry Sauce:
- In a small bowl, mix together curry powder, ground cumin, ground coriander, turmeric, cayenne pepper, salt, and black pepper.

- Sprinkle the spice mixture over the vegetables and chickpeas. Stir to coat evenly.

Pour in Coconut Milk:
- Pour the coconut milk into the skillet. Stir well to combine all the ingredients.

Simmer:
- Bring the curry to a gentle simmer. Reduce the heat to low and let it simmer for 15-20 minutes, allowing the flavors to meld and the vegetables to become tender.

Adjust Seasoning:
- Taste the curry and adjust the seasoning, adding more salt or spices if needed.

Serve:
- Serve the Chickpea and Vegetable Curry over cooked rice or with naan bread.

Garnish:
- Garnish with chopped fresh cilantro before serving.

Enjoy:
- Enjoy your delicious and flavorful Chickpea and Vegetable Curry!

This curry is not only satisfying and hearty but also vegetarian-friendly. Feel free to customize the vegetables or spice level according to your preferences. It's a perfect dish for a cozy and flavorful meal.

Side Dishes:

Roasted Sweet Potato Wedges

Ingredients:

- 2 large sweet potatoes, washed and scrubbed
- 2 tablespoons olive oil
- 1 teaspoon paprika
- 1 teaspoon garlic powder
- 1/2 teaspoon cumin
- 1/2 teaspoon cinnamon (optional)
- Salt and black pepper, to taste
- Fresh parsley, chopped, for garnish (optional)

Instructions:

Preheat the Oven:
- Preheat your oven to 425°F (220°C).

Prepare the Sweet Potatoes:
- Cut the sweet potatoes into wedges. You can leave the skin on for added texture and nutrients.

Coat with Olive Oil and Spices:
- In a large bowl, toss the sweet potato wedges with olive oil, paprika, garlic powder, cumin, cinnamon (if using), salt, and black pepper. Make sure the wedges are well coated.

Arrange on Baking Sheet:
- Arrange the seasoned sweet potato wedges in a single layer on a baking sheet. This helps them cook evenly.

Roast in the Oven:
- Roast the sweet potato wedges in the preheated oven for 25-30 minutes or until they are golden brown and crispy on the edges. Flip the wedges halfway through the cooking time for even roasting.

Garnish and Serve:
- Once the sweet potato wedges are done, remove them from the oven. Garnish with chopped fresh parsley if desired.

Enjoy:
- Serve the Roasted Sweet Potato Wedges hot as a delicious and healthy side dish.

These sweet potato wedges make a flavorful and nutritious snack or side dish. The combination of spices adds a savory and aromatic touch, while the roasting process enhances the natural sweetness of the sweet potatoes. They pair well with various dipping sauces or can be enjoyed on their own.

Quinoa Pilaf with Mixed Vegetables

Ingredients:

- 1 cup quinoa, rinsed and drained
- 2 cups vegetable broth or water
- 1 tablespoon olive oil
- 1 onion, finely chopped
- 2 cloves garlic, minced
- 1 carrot, diced
- 1 zucchini, diced
- 1 bell pepper (any color), diced
- 1 cup broccoli florets
- 1 teaspoon ground cumin
- 1/2 teaspoon ground coriander
- Salt and black pepper, to taste
- 1/4 cup fresh parsley, chopped (for garnish)
- Lemon wedges, for serving

Instructions:

Rinse Quinoa:
- Rinse quinoa under cold water until the water runs clear. This helps remove any bitter coating.

Cook Quinoa:
- In a medium saucepan, combine quinoa and vegetable broth or water. Bring to a boil, then reduce the heat to low, cover, and simmer for 15-20 minutes, or until the quinoa is cooked and the liquid is absorbed. Fluff the quinoa with a fork.

Saute Vegetables:
- In a large skillet, heat olive oil over medium heat. Add chopped onion and sauté until softened.
- Add minced garlic, diced carrot, diced zucchini, diced bell pepper, and broccoli florets to the skillet. Sauté for about 5-7 minutes or until the vegetables are tender-crisp.

Combine Quinoa and Vegetables:
- Add the cooked quinoa to the skillet with the sautéed vegetables. Mix well to combine.

Season the Pilaf:
- Sprinkle ground cumin, ground coriander, salt, and black pepper over the quinoa and vegetables. Stir to evenly distribute the seasonings.

Garnish and Serve:

- Garnish the quinoa pilaf with chopped fresh parsley.

Serve with Lemon Wedges:
- Serve the quinoa pilaf hot, and provide lemon wedges on the side for a burst of citrus flavor.

Enjoy:
- Enjoy your Quinoa Pilaf with Mixed Vegetables as a wholesome and satisfying dish!

This quinoa pilaf is not only flavorful but also versatile. Feel free to customize it by adding your favorite herbs, spices, or additional vegetables. It makes a delicious and nutritious side dish or a light and wholesome meal on its own.

Steamed Broccoli with a Squeeze of Lemon

Ingredients:

- 1 pound (about 450g) broccoli florets, washed and trimmed
- 1 tablespoon olive oil (optional)
- Salt, to taste
- Freshly ground black pepper, to taste
- 1 lemon, cut into wedges

Instructions:

Prepare the Broccoli:
- Wash the broccoli florets and trim them into bite-sized pieces.

Steam the Broccoli:
- Place a steamer basket in a pot with a few inches of water. Bring the water to a simmer over medium heat.
- Add the broccoli florets to the steamer basket. Cover the pot and steam the broccoli for about 3-5 minutes or until it is crisp-tender. Be careful not to overcook, as you want the broccoli to retain its bright green color and a slight crunch.

Season the Broccoli:
- Once the broccoli is steamed, transfer it to a serving bowl. Drizzle olive oil over the broccoli if desired (this step is optional but adds extra flavor).
- Sprinkle salt and freshly ground black pepper over the steamed broccoli. Toss gently to evenly coat the broccoli with the seasoning.

Squeeze of Lemon:
- Squeeze fresh lemon juice over the steamed broccoli. The lemon adds a refreshing citrus flavor that enhances the taste of the broccoli.

Serve:
- Serve the Steamed Broccoli with a Squeeze of Lemon immediately.

Enjoy:
- Enjoy your simple, healthy, and flavorful side dish!

This recipe is a quick and nutritious way to enjoy broccoli. The combination of steaming, olive oil, and a squeeze of lemon elevates the flavors, making it a delicious and vibrant side dish. Adjust the seasoning and lemon juice according to your taste preferences.

Pasta:

Whole Wheat Pasta with Tomato and Basil Sauce

Ingredients:

- 8 oz (about 225g) whole wheat pasta
- 2 tablespoons olive oil
- 1 onion, finely chopped
- 3 cloves garlic, minced
- 1 can (28 oz) crushed tomatoes
- 1 teaspoon dried oregano
- 1 teaspoon dried basil
- 1/2 teaspoon red pepper flakes (optional, for heat)
- Salt and black pepper, to taste
- Fresh basil leaves, chopped, for garnish
- Grated Parmesan cheese, for serving (optional)

Instructions:

Cook the Whole Wheat Pasta:
- Cook the whole wheat pasta according to the package instructions in a large pot of salted boiling water. Drain and set aside.

Prepare the Tomato and Basil Sauce:
- In a large skillet, heat olive oil over medium heat. Add chopped onion and sauté until softened.
- Add minced garlic and sauté for an additional 1-2 minutes until fragrant.
- Pour in the crushed tomatoes and add dried oregano, dried basil, red pepper flakes (if using), salt, and black pepper. Stir to combine.

Simmer the Sauce:
- Bring the tomato and basil sauce to a simmer. Reduce the heat to low and let it simmer for about 15-20 minutes, stirring occasionally. This allows the flavors to meld and the sauce to thicken.

Combine Pasta and Sauce:
- Add the cooked whole wheat pasta to the skillet with the tomato and basil sauce. Toss until the pasta is well coated with the sauce.

Garnish and Serve:
- Garnish the pasta with freshly chopped basil leaves.

Optional: Serve with Parmesan Cheese:

- If desired, serve the Whole Wheat Pasta with Tomato and Basil Sauce with grated Parmesan cheese on top.

Enjoy:
- Enjoy your wholesome and delicious Whole Wheat Pasta with Tomato and Basil Sauce!

This recipe is a healthier twist on traditional pasta dishes, thanks to the use of whole wheat pasta. The tomato and basil sauce provides a classic and fresh flavor combination. Feel free to customize the recipe by adding your favorite vegetables or adjusting the seasonings according to your taste preferences.

Zucchini Noodles with Marinara Sauce

Ingredients:

For the Zucchini Noodles:

- 4 medium-sized zucchini
- Salt, for seasoning

For the Marinara Sauce:

- 2 tablespoons olive oil
- 1 onion, finely chopped
- 3 cloves garlic, minced
- 1 can (28 oz) crushed tomatoes
- 1 teaspoon dried oregano
- 1 teaspoon dried basil
- 1/2 teaspoon red pepper flakes (optional, for heat)
- Salt and black pepper, to taste
- Fresh basil leaves, chopped, for garnish (optional)
- Grated Parmesan cheese, for serving (optional)

Instructions:

1. Prepare the Zucchini Noodles:

    Using a spiralizer, spiralize the zucchini into noodle shapes. If you don't have a spiralizer, you can use a vegetable peeler to create thin strips or julienne the zucchini into long, thin strands.
    Place the zucchini noodles in a colander, sprinkle with salt, and let them sit for about 15-20 minutes. This helps draw out excess moisture. Rinse the noodles under cold water and pat them dry with a paper towel.

2. Make the Marinara Sauce:

    In a large skillet, heat olive oil over medium heat. Add chopped onion and sauté until softened.
    Add minced garlic and sauté for an additional 1-2 minutes until fragrant.
    Pour in the crushed tomatoes and add dried oregano, dried basil, red pepper flakes (if using), salt, and black pepper. Stir to combine.

Bring the marinara sauce to a simmer, then reduce the heat to low and let it simmer for about 15-20 minutes, stirring occasionally. Adjust the seasoning to taste.

3. Cook the Zucchini Noodles:

In a separate large skillet, heat a bit of olive oil over medium heat.
Add the prepared zucchini noodles and toss them for 2-3 minutes until they are just tender but still have a slight crunch.

4. Combine and Serve:

Pour the marinara sauce over the cooked zucchini noodles and toss until the noodles are evenly coated.
Garnish with chopped fresh basil if desired.

5. Optional: Serve with Parmesan Cheese:

- If desired, serve the Zucchini Noodles with Marinara Sauce with grated Parmesan cheese on top.

6. Enjoy:

- Enjoy your healthy and delicious Zucchini Noodles with Marinara Sauce!

This recipe is a great low-carb and gluten-free alternative to traditional pasta dishes. The fresh and vibrant flavors of the marinara sauce complement the light and tender zucchini noodles. Feel free to customize the recipe with additional herbs, vegetables, or protein of your choice.

Shrimp and Vegetable Pasta with a Light Garlic Sauce

Ingredients:

- 8 oz (about 225g) whole wheat or your preferred pasta
- 1 pound (about 450g) large shrimp, peeled and deveined
- 2 tablespoons olive oil
- 3 cloves garlic, minced
- 1 zucchini, thinly sliced
- 1 bell pepper (any color), thinly sliced
- 1 cup cherry tomatoes, halved
- 1/2 cup baby spinach leaves
- 1/2 cup chicken or vegetable broth
- 1 tablespoon lemon juice
- 1 teaspoon lemon zest
- 1/2 teaspoon red pepper flakes (optional, for heat)
- Salt and black pepper, to taste
- Fresh parsley, chopped, for garnish
- Grated Parmesan cheese, for serving (optional)

Instructions:

    Cook the Pasta:
- Cook the pasta according to the package instructions in a large pot of salted boiling water. Drain and set aside.

    Prepare the Shrimp:
- Season the shrimp with salt and black pepper. In a large skillet, heat 1 tablespoon of olive oil over medium-high heat. Add the shrimp and cook for 2-3 minutes per side or until they are pink and opaque. Remove the shrimp from the skillet and set aside.

    Saute Vegetables:
- In the same skillet, add the remaining 1 tablespoon of olive oil. Add minced garlic and sauté for about 30 seconds until fragrant.
- Add sliced zucchini, sliced bell pepper, and cherry tomatoes to the skillet. Cook for 3-4 minutes or until the vegetables are tender-crisp.

    Make the Garlic Sauce:
- Pour in chicken or vegetable broth, lemon juice, lemon zest, and red pepper flakes (if using). Stir well to combine and let it simmer for 2 minutes.

Combine Pasta, Shrimp, and Vegetables:
- Add the cooked pasta, cooked shrimp, and baby spinach to the skillet. Toss everything together until well combined and heated through.

Adjust Seasoning:
- Taste and adjust the seasoning with salt and black pepper if needed.

Garnish and Serve:
- Garnish the Shrimp and Vegetable Pasta with chopped fresh parsley.

Optional: Serve with Parmesan Cheese:
- If desired, serve the pasta with grated Parmesan cheese on top.

Enjoy:
- Serve your delicious Shrimp and Vegetable Pasta with a Light Garlic Sauce hot and enjoy!

This recipe offers a light and flavorful garlic sauce that complements the shrimp and vegetables. It's a quick and satisfying dish that can be customized with your favorite vegetables and herbs. Feel free to experiment and make it your own!

Grains:

Brown Rice with Black Beans and Corn

Ingredients:

- 1 cup brown rice
- 2 cups water
- 1 can (15 oz) black beans, drained and rinsed
- 1 cup corn kernels (fresh, frozen, or canned)
- 1 tablespoon olive oil
- 1 onion, finely chopped
- 2 cloves garlic, minced
- 1 teaspoon ground cumin
- 1 teaspoon chili powder
- 1/2 teaspoon smoked paprika
- Salt and black pepper, to taste
- Fresh cilantro, chopped, for garnish (optional)
- Lime wedges, for serving

Instructions:

1. Cook Brown Rice:

    Rinse the brown rice under cold water.
    In a medium saucepan, combine the rinsed rice with 2 cups of water. Bring to a boil.
    Reduce the heat to low, cover, and simmer for about 45-50 minutes or until the rice is tender and water is absorbed.
    Fluff the cooked rice with a fork.

2. Saute Onions and Garlic:

    In a large skillet, heat olive oil over medium heat.
    Add finely chopped onions and sauté until they are softened.
    Add minced garlic and sauté for an additional 1-2 minutes until fragrant.

3. Add Black Beans and Corn:

Add drained and rinsed black beans to the skillet, followed by corn kernels.
Stir to combine and heat through.

4. Season with Spices:

    Sprinkle ground cumin, chili powder, smoked paprika, salt, and black pepper over the beans and corn mixture.
    Stir well to evenly coat the beans and corn with the spices.

5. Combine with Brown Rice:

    Add the cooked brown rice to the skillet with the black beans and corn.
    Mix everything together until well combined.

6. Garnish and Serve:

    Garnish with chopped fresh cilantro if desired.
    Serve the Brown Rice with Black Beans and Corn hot, and provide lime wedges on the side for squeezing over the dish.

7. Enjoy:

Enjoy your nutritious and flavorful Brown Rice with Black Beans and Corn! This dish is not only delicious but also rich in protein and fiber. It makes for a satisfying and wholesome meal, and you can customize it with your favorite toppings or additional vegetables.

Barley and Vegetable Stir-Fry

Ingredients:

- 1 cup barley
- 2 cups water
- 2 tablespoons vegetable oil
- 1 onion, thinly sliced
- 2 carrots, julienned
- 1 bell pepper (any color), thinly sliced
- 1 zucchini, thinly sliced
- 1 cup broccoli florets
- 3 cloves garlic, minced
- 1 tablespoon soy sauce
- 1 tablespoon hoisin sauce
- 1 tablespoon rice vinegar
- 1 teaspoon sesame oil
- 1 teaspoon grated fresh ginger
- Salt and black pepper, to taste
- Green onions, chopped, for garnish
- Sesame seeds, for garnish (optional)

Instructions:

1. Cook Barley:

    Rinse the barley under cold water.
    In a medium saucepan, combine the rinsed barley with 2 cups of water. Bring to a boil.
    Reduce the heat to low, cover, and simmer for about 40-45 minutes or until the barley is tender but still has a slight chewiness.
    Drain any excess water and set the cooked barley aside.

2. Prepare Vegetables:

    Heat vegetable oil in a large wok or skillet over medium-high heat.

Add sliced onions, julienned carrots, sliced bell pepper, sliced zucchini, and broccoli florets. Stir-fry for 5-7 minutes or until the vegetables are tender-crisp.

3. Add Garlic and Barley:

Add minced garlic to the vegetables and stir-fry for an additional 1-2 minutes until fragrant.
Add the cooked barley to the wok and toss everything together.

4. Prepare Stir-Fry Sauce:

In a small bowl, whisk together soy sauce, hoisin sauce, rice vinegar, sesame oil, and grated fresh ginger.

5. Combine with Sauce:

Pour the stir-fry sauce over the barley and vegetables.
Toss everything to ensure the barley and vegetables are well coated with the sauce.

6. Season and Garnish:

Season with salt and black pepper to taste.
Garnish with chopped green onions and sesame seeds if desired.

7. Serve:

Serve the Barley and Vegetable Stir-Fry hot and enjoy this hearty and nutritious dish!

Feel free to customize this stir-fry by adding your favorite vegetables or adjusting the sauce ingredients to your taste preferences. It's a great way to enjoy a variety of veggies and incorporate the chewy texture of barley into your meal.

Bulgur Wheat Salad with Herbs and Cherry Tomatoes

Ingredients:

- 1 cup coarse bulgur wheat
- 1 1/2 cups boiling water
- 1 cup cherry tomatoes, halved
- 1 cucumber, diced
- 1/2 red onion, finely chopped
- 1/2 cup fresh parsley, chopped
- 1/4 cup fresh mint, chopped
- 1/4 cup extra-virgin olive oil
- 3 tablespoons lemon juice
- Salt and black pepper, to taste
- Feta cheese, crumbled, for garnish (optional)

Instructions:

1. Prepare Bulgur Wheat:

    Place the bulgur wheat in a large heatproof bowl.
    Pour boiling water over the bulgur wheat, ensuring it is fully covered.
    Cover the bowl with a lid or plastic wrap and let it sit for about 20-25 minutes or until the bulgur is tender and has absorbed the water.

2. Fluff Bulgur and Cool:

    Once the bulgur is tender, fluff it with a fork to separate the grains.
    Allow the bulgur to cool to room temperature.

3. Assemble the Salad:

    In a large mixing bowl, combine the cooled bulgur wheat, cherry tomatoes, diced cucumber, finely chopped red onion, fresh parsley, and fresh mint.

4. Prepare the Dressing:

    In a small bowl, whisk together extra-virgin olive oil and lemon juice.
    Season the dressing with salt and black pepper to taste.

5. Combine Salad with Dressing:

   Pour the dressing over the bulgur and vegetable mixture.
   Toss everything together until well coated with the dressing.

6. Garnish and Serve:

   Garnish the Bulgur Wheat Salad with crumbled feta cheese if desired.
   Serve the salad immediately or refrigerate for a few hours to allow the flavors to meld.

7. Enjoy:

Enjoy your refreshing Bulgur Wheat Salad with Herbs and Cherry Tomatoes! This salad is a light and nutritious dish, perfect for a side dish or a light meal on its own. Feel free to customize it by adding other fresh vegetables or your favorite herbs.

Desserts:

Mixed Berry Sorbet

Ingredients:

- 3 cups mixed berries (such as strawberries, blueberries, raspberries, and blackberries)
- 1/2 cup granulated sugar
- 1 tablespoon fresh lemon juice
- 1/2 cup water

Instructions:

1. Prepare the Berries:

    Rinse the mixed berries under cold water.
    Remove any stems or hulls from strawberries.

2. Make Simple Syrup:

    In a small saucepan, combine granulated sugar and water.
    Heat over medium heat, stirring occasionally, until the sugar dissolves completely.
    Remove the simple syrup from heat and let it cool to room temperature.

3. Blend the Berries:

    In a blender or food processor, combine the mixed berries and fresh lemon juice.
    Blend until the berries are pureed and smooth.

4. Strain (Optional):

    If you prefer a smoother sorbet, you can strain the berry mixture through a fine-mesh sieve to remove seeds and pulp. Press the mixture with the back of a spoon to extract as much liquid as possible.

5. Combine with Simple Syrup:

    Combine the berry puree with the cooled simple syrup.
    Stir well to ensure the sugar syrup is evenly mixed with the berry mixture.

6. Chill:

    Refrigerate the mixture for at least 2-3 hours to chill thoroughly.

7. Churn in Ice Cream Maker:

    Transfer the chilled mixture to an ice cream maker.
    Churn according to the manufacturer's instructions until you achieve a sorbet-like consistency.

8. Freeze:

    If the sorbet is too soft, transfer it to an airtight container and freeze for an additional 2-3 hours or until firm.

9. Serve:

    Scoop the Mixed Berry Sorbet into bowls or cones.
    Garnish with additional fresh berries if desired.

10. Enjoy:

Enjoy your homemade Mixed Berry Sorbet as a refreshing and fruity treat! This sorbet is a perfect way to enjoy the natural sweetness of mixed berries without added preservatives or artificial flavors.

Angel Food Cake with Fresh Strawberries

Ingredients:

For the Angel Food Cake:

- 1 cup cake flour
- 1 1/2 cups granulated sugar
- 12 large egg whites, at room temperature
- 1 1/2 teaspoons cream of tartar
- 1/4 teaspoon salt
- 1 teaspoon vanilla extract
- 1/2 teaspoon almond extract

For the Fresh Strawberries:

- 2 cups fresh strawberries, hulled and sliced
- 2 tablespoons granulated sugar
- 1 teaspoon fresh lemon juice

For Serving (Optional):

- Whipped cream
- Mint leaves for garnish

Instructions:

For the Angel Food Cake:

Preheat the Oven:
- Preheat your oven to 350°F (175°C).

Prepare the Cake Pan:
- Use a tube pan (angel food cake pan) and do not grease it. The cake needs to cling to the sides to rise properly.

Sift the Flour:
- Sift cake flour and 3/4 cup of granulated sugar together three times to ensure it is well combined and aerated.

Whip the Egg Whites:
- In a large bowl, beat the egg whites with an electric mixer on medium speed until foamy.

- Add cream of tartar and salt, and continue beating until soft peaks form.
- Gradually add the remaining 3/4 cup of granulated sugar, about 2 tablespoons at a time, beating on high speed until stiff, glossy peaks form.

Add Extracts:
- Gently fold in vanilla extract and almond extract.

Add Flour Mixture:
- Gradually sift the flour mixture over the whipped egg whites, about 1/4 cup at a time, and gently fold in until just combined. Be careful not to deflate the egg whites.

Bake:
- Spoon the batter into the ungreased tube pan. Smooth the top with a spatula.
- Bake in the preheated oven for 35-40 minutes or until the top springs back when lightly touched.
- Invert the pan onto a cooling rack immediately after removing it from the oven. Allow it to cool completely.

Release Cake:
- Once the cake is completely cool, run a knife around the edges of the pan and the center tube to release the cake.

For the Fresh Strawberries:

Prepare the Strawberries:
- In a bowl, combine sliced strawberries, granulated sugar, and fresh lemon juice. Toss gently to coat the strawberries in sugar.
- Let the strawberries sit for about 15-20 minutes to allow them to release their juices and become slightly syrupy.

For Serving:

Slice and Serve:
- Slice the angel food cake and serve it topped with the macerated strawberries.

Optional: Add Whipped Cream:
- Serve with a dollop of whipped cream on top, and garnish with mint leaves if desired.

Enjoy:
- Enjoy your light and airy Angel Food Cake with Fresh Strawberries!

This classic dessert is perfect for a light and summery treat. The combination of fluffy angel food cake and sweet, juicy strawberries is a delightful way to celebrate the season.

Baked Apples with Cinnamon and a Sprinkle of Oats

Ingredients:

- 4 medium-sized apples (such as Granny Smith or Honeycrisp)
- 2 tablespoons unsalted butter, melted
- 2 tablespoons brown sugar
- 1 teaspoon ground cinnamon
- 1/4 cup old-fashioned oats
- 1/4 cup chopped nuts (such as walnuts or pecans), optional
- Vanilla ice cream or whipped cream for serving (optional)

Instructions:

Preheat the Oven:
- Preheat your oven to 375°F (190°C).

Prepare the Apples:
- Wash and core the apples. You can use an apple corer or simply cut out the core with a knife, leaving the bottom intact.

Mix the Filling:
- In a small bowl, mix together melted butter, brown sugar, and ground cinnamon.

Fill the Apples:
- Place the cored apples in a baking dish.
- Spoon the butter, sugar, and cinnamon mixture into each apple, distributing it evenly.

Sprinkle with Oats:
- Sprinkle old-fashioned oats over the top of each filled apple.

Optional: Add Nuts:
- If you like, add chopped nuts over the oats for added crunch and flavor.

Bake:
- Bake the apples in the preheated oven for about 25-30 minutes or until the apples are tender and the tops are golden brown.

Serve:
- Remove the baked apples from the oven and let them cool for a few minutes.
- Serve the baked apples warm.

Optional: Serve with Ice Cream or Whipped Cream:

- For an extra treat, serve the baked apples with a scoop of vanilla ice cream or a dollop of whipped cream.

Enjoy:
- Enjoy your delicious Baked Apples with Cinnamon and a Sprinkle of Oats!

This simple dessert brings out the natural sweetness of the apples, enhanced by the warm cinnamon and crunchy oats. It's a comforting and wholesome treat, perfect for a cozy dessert or a sweet ending to a fall or winter meal.

Snacks:

Air-Popped Popcorn with a Dash of Nutritional Yeast

Ingredients:

- 1/2 cup popcorn kernels
- 1-2 tablespoons nutritional yeast
- Salt, to taste (optional)
- 1-2 tablespoons melted butter or olive oil (optional)

Instructions:

Pop the Popcorn:
- Use an air popper to pop the popcorn kernels. If you don't have an air popper, you can pop the corn using your preferred method.

Season with Nutritional Yeast:
- Transfer the freshly popped popcorn to a large bowl.
- Sprinkle 1-2 tablespoons of nutritional yeast over the popcorn. Nutritional yeast adds a cheesy and savory flavor to the popcorn.

Optional: Add Salt:
- If desired, sprinkle a bit of salt over the popcorn. Adjust the amount to your taste preferences.

Optional: Drizzle with Butter or Olive Oil:
- For added richness, you can drizzle melted butter or olive oil over the popcorn. Toss the popcorn to ensure an even coating.

Toss and Mix:
- Toss the popcorn gently to mix the nutritional yeast, salt, and optional butter or olive oil evenly.

Serve:
- Serve your Air-Popped Popcorn with a Dash of Nutritional Yeast immediately.

Enjoy:
- Enjoy your delicious and nutritious popcorn snack!

This recipe is a healthier alternative to traditional buttered popcorn, and the nutritional yeast adds a unique flavor that's reminiscent of cheese. It's a great way to enjoy a savory and satisfying snack without a lot of added calories. Feel free to experiment with the seasoning to suit your taste preferences!

Fresh Fruit Salad

Ingredients:

- 2 cups watermelon, cubed
- 1 cup pineapple, cubed
- 1 cup grapes, halved
- 1 cup strawberries, hulled and sliced
- 1 cup kiwi, peeled and diced
- 1 cup blueberries
- 1 cup mango, peeled and diced
- 1 banana, sliced
- Fresh mint leaves, for garnish (optional)

For the Citrus Dressing:

- 2 tablespoons honey or maple syrup
- 2 tablespoons freshly squeezed orange juice
- 1 tablespoon freshly squeezed lemon juice
- 1 teaspoon lime juice (optional)
- Zest of one orange (optional)

Instructions:

Prepare the Fruits:
- Wash and prepare all the fruits as directed. Ensure that they are well-drained.

Combine Fruits:
- In a large mixing bowl, combine watermelon, pineapple, grapes, strawberries, kiwi, blueberries, mango, and banana.

Prepare the Citrus Dressing:
- In a small bowl, whisk together honey or maple syrup, orange juice, lemon juice, lime juice (if using), and orange zest (if using). Mix until well combined.

Pour Dressing Over Fruits:
- Pour the citrus dressing over the mixed fruits.

Gently Toss:
- Gently toss the fruits with the dressing until they are well coated.

Chill (Optional):
- If time allows, refrigerate the fruit salad for about 30 minutes to let the flavors meld and the salad chill.

Garnish and Serve:
- Before serving, garnish the fresh fruit salad with fresh mint leaves if desired.

Enjoy:
- Serve the Fresh Fruit Salad and enjoy this vibrant and healthy treat!

This fruit salad is not only visually appealing but also a nutritious and delicious way to enjoy a variety of fresh fruits. Feel free to customize the fruit selection based on what's in season or your personal preferences. It makes for a perfect side dish, snack, or even a light dessert.

Greek Yogurt with a Drizzle of Honey

Ingredients:

- 1 cup Greek yogurt (plain, unsweetened)
- 1-2 tablespoons honey (adjust to taste)
- Optional toppings: fresh fruits, nuts, or granola

Instructions:

Prepare the Greek Yogurt:

- Measure out 1 cup of plain Greek yogurt and place it in a bowl.

Drizzle with Honey:

- Use a spoon to drizzle 1 to 2 tablespoons of honey over the Greek yogurt. You can adjust the amount of honey based on your sweetness preference.

Mix It Up:

- Gently stir the honey into the Greek yogurt until it is well combined. This will create a sweet and creamy mixture.

Optional Toppings:

- Enhance your Greek yogurt with additional toppings for extra flavor and texture. Consider adding fresh fruits like berries, banana slices, or chopped mango. You can also sprinkle some nuts (such as almonds or walnuts) or a handful of granola for a crunchy element.

Serve and Enjoy:

- Transfer the Greek yogurt mixture to a serving bowl or enjoy it directly from the bowl. It's a versatile recipe that can be eaten as a quick snack, a healthy dessert, or a satisfying breakfast.

Feel free to get creative with the toppings based on your preferences. This recipe provides a balanced combination of protein from the Greek yogurt and natural sweetness from the honey, making it a nutritious and tasty treat.

Beverages:

Infused Water with Cucumber and Mint

Ingredients:

- 1 cucumber, washed and sliced
- 1 bunch of fresh mint leaves, washed
- 1-2 liters of water (depending on the size of your pitcher)
- Ice cubes (optional)

Instructions:

Prepare the Ingredients:
- Wash the cucumber thoroughly and slice it into thin rounds.
- Wash the fresh mint leaves and pat them dry.

Combine Cucumber and Mint:
- In a large pitcher, combine the cucumber slices and fresh mint leaves. The combination of cucumber and mint adds a crisp and cool flavor to the water.

Add Water:
- Pour 1-2 liters of water into the pitcher, depending on the size of your container. Use filtered or chilled water for the best taste.

Refrigerate:
- Place the pitcher in the refrigerator and let it sit for at least 2-4 hours to allow the flavors to infuse. For a stronger flavor, you can refrigerate it overnight.

Serve:

- When ready to serve, you can strain the infused water to remove the cucumber and mint pieces, or you can leave them in the pitcher for a more visually appealing presentation.

Add Ice Cubes (Optional):

- If you like your infused water extra cold, you can add ice cubes to the pitcher or pour the infused water over ice when serving.

Garnish (Optional):

- For a decorative touch, you can garnish individual glasses with a slice of cucumber or a sprig of fresh mint.

Enjoy:

- Pour yourself a glass of this refreshing cucumber and mint infused water and enjoy a flavorful, hydrating drink without any added sugars.

Feel free to customize this recipe by adding other fruits or herbs, such as lemon slices, lime wedges, or even a few berries, to create your own unique infused water blend. It's a healthy and delightful alternative to sugary drinks.

Iced Green Tea with Lemon

Ingredients:

- 2 green tea bags
- 4 cups water
- 1-2 lemons, sliced
- Ice cubes
- Optional: Mint leaves, honey or sweetener of your choice

Instructions:

Brew Green Tea:
- Bring 4 cups of water to a boil. Once the water is boiling, remove it from heat and add the green tea bags. Allow the tea to steep for 3-5 minutes, or according to the instructions on the tea bag.

Sweeten (Optional):
- If you prefer sweetened iced tea, you can add honey or your preferred sweetener to the hot tea while it's steeping. Stir well to dissolve the sweetener.

Cool the Tea:
- Once the tea has steeped, remove the tea bags and let the tea cool to room temperature. You can speed up the cooling process by placing the tea in the refrigerator.

Prepare Lemon Slices:
- While the tea is cooling, slice the lemons into thin rounds. You can also squeeze some lemon juice into the tea for extra citrus flavor.

Assemble Iced Tea:

- Fill a pitcher with ice cubes. Pour the cooled green tea over the ice.

Add Lemon Slices:

- Drop the lemon slices into the pitcher of iced tea. This will infuse the tea with a refreshing citrus flavor.

Optional Mint Garnish:

- If you like, you can add a few fresh mint leaves to the pitcher for a hint of minty freshness.

Stir and Serve:

- Give the iced green tea a gentle stir to mix the flavors. You can also add more ice if needed.

Serve with Lemon Wedges (Optional):

- To enhance the presentation, you can serve the iced green tea in glasses with a wedge of lemon on the rim.

Enjoy:

- Pour yourself a glass of this delicious iced green tea with lemon and enjoy a refreshing and hydrating drink.

This iced green tea is a wonderful way to enjoy the health benefits of green tea in a cool and flavorful form. Adjust the sweetness and lemon intensity to suit your taste preferences.

Berry Smoothie with Low-Fat Milk or Yogurt

Ingredients:

- 1 cup mixed berries (strawberries, blueberries, raspberries, or blackberries)
- 1/2 banana (optional, for added creaminess)
- 1 cup low-fat milk or low-fat yogurt
- 1 tablespoon honey or maple syrup (optional, for added sweetness)
- Ice cubes (optional)

Instructions:

Prepare the Berries:
- Wash the berries thoroughly. If you're using strawberries, hull and chop them.

Banana (Optional):
- If you like your smoothie creamier, add half a banana. Bananas add sweetness and a creamy texture to the smoothie.

Combine Ingredients:
- In a blender, combine the mixed berries, banana (if using), low-fat milk or yogurt, and honey or maple syrup (if using).

Blend Until Smooth:
- Blend the ingredients until smooth and creamy. If the consistency is too thick, you can add more milk or yogurt to achieve your desired thickness.

Taste and Adjust:
- Taste the smoothie and adjust the sweetness by adding more honey or maple syrup if needed.

Add Ice Cubes (Optional):

- If you prefer a colder smoothie, you can add a handful of ice cubes to the blender and blend again until smooth.

Pour and Serve:

- Pour the berry smoothie into glasses and serve immediately.

Garnish (Optional):

- Garnish the smoothie with a few whole berries or a mint sprig for a decorative touch.

Enjoy:

- Sip and enjoy your delicious and nutritious berry smoothie!

Feel free to customize the recipe by using different berries or adjusting the sweetness to suit your taste. This smoothie is a great way to incorporate vitamins, antioxidants, and protein into your diet while enjoying a tasty and satisfying drink.

Grilled Options:

Grilled Vegetable Skewers

Ingredients:

- 1 zucchini, sliced into rounds
- 1 yellow bell pepper, cut into chunks
- 1 red bell pepper, cut into chunks
- 1 red onion, cut into chunks
- 1 eggplant, cut into cubes
- 1 cup cherry tomatoes
- 8-10 button mushrooms, cleaned
- 3 tablespoons olive oil
- 2 tablespoons balsamic vinegar
- 2 cloves garlic, minced
- 1 teaspoon dried thyme
- 1 teaspoon dried rosemary
- Salt and pepper, to taste
- Wooden or metal skewers

Instructions:

Preheat the Grill:
- Preheat your grill to medium-high heat.

Prepare the Vegetables:

- Wash and chop the vegetables into bite-sized pieces. Keep the cherry tomatoes and mushrooms whole.

Prepare the Marinade:

- In a bowl, whisk together the olive oil, balsamic vinegar, minced garlic, dried thyme, dried rosemary, salt, and pepper.

Marinate the Vegetables:

- Toss the chopped vegetables in the marinade, making sure they are well-coated. Allow them to marinate for at least 15-30 minutes to absorb the flavors.

Skewer the Vegetables:

- Thread the marinated vegetables onto skewers, alternating between different types of vegetables. This helps ensure even cooking.

Grill the Skewers:

- Place the vegetable skewers on the preheated grill. Grill for about 12-15 minutes, turning occasionally, until the vegetables are tender and have nice grill marks.

Baste with Marinade (Optional):

- Optionally, you can baste the skewers with any remaining marinade during the grilling process for added flavor.

Serve Hot:

- Once the vegetable skewers are grilled to perfection, remove them from the grill and transfer them to a serving plate.

Garnish (Optional):

- Garnish with fresh herbs like parsley or basil before serving.

Enjoy:

- Serve the grilled vegetable skewers as a side dish, appetizer, or alongside your favorite main course. They are great for outdoor gatherings and barbecue parties.

Feel free to experiment with different herbs, spices, or additional vegetables to suit your taste preferences. These grilled vegetable skewers are not only delicious but also a healthy and colorful addition to your meal.

Turkey burgers with Lean Ground Turkey

Ingredients:

- 1 pound lean ground turkey
- 1/4 cup breadcrumbs (whole wheat for a healthier option)
- 1/4 cup finely chopped onion
- 1/4 cup finely chopped parsley
- 1 clove garlic, minced
- 1 teaspoon Dijon mustard
- 1 teaspoon Worcestershire sauce
- 1/2 teaspoon salt
- 1/4 teaspoon black pepper
- Olive oil (for brushing the grill or pan)
- Whole grain burger buns
- Toppings and condiments of your choice (lettuce, tomato, onion, pickles, mustard, ketchup, etc.)

Instructions:

Preheat the Grill or Pan:
- Preheat your grill or stovetop pan over medium-high heat.

Prepare the Turkey Burger Mixture:
- In a large bowl, combine the lean ground turkey, breadcrumbs, chopped onion, chopped parsley, minced garlic, Dijon mustard, Worcestershire sauce, salt, and black pepper. Mix the ingredients until well combined.

Form Burger Patties:

- Divide the turkey mixture into equal portions and shape them into burger patties. Aim for patties that are about 1/2 to 3/4 inch thick for even cooking.

Brush with Olive Oil:

- Brush the grill grates or the pan with a bit of olive oil to prevent sticking.

Grill or Pan-Cook the Turkey Burgers:

- Place the turkey burgers on the preheated grill or pan. Cook for about 5-6 minutes per side, or until the internal temperature reaches 165°F (74°C) and the burgers are cooked through.

Toast the Buns (Optional):

- If you like, you can toast the whole grain burger buns on the grill or in a toaster for a minute or two.

Assemble the Burgers:

- Place the cooked turkey burgers on the toasted buns. Add your favorite toppings and condiments.

Serve:

- Serve the turkey burgers hot with a side of salad, sweet potato fries, or your preferred side dish.

Enjoy:

- Enjoy your delicious and lean turkey burgers!

Feel free to customize the recipe by adding herbs, spices, or other ingredients that you enjoy. These turkey burgers are a healthier option and can be a flavorful and satisfying meal for lunch or dinner.

Portobello Mushroom Burgers

Ingredients:

- 4 large Portobello mushrooms, stems removed
- 2 tablespoons balsamic vinegar
- 2 tablespoons soy sauce or tamari (for a gluten-free option)
- 2 tablespoons olive oil
- 2 cloves garlic, minced
- 1 teaspoon dried thyme
- Salt and black pepper, to taste
- 4 whole grain burger buns
- Toppings and condiments of your choice (lettuce, tomato, onion, avocado, vegan mayo, etc.)

Instructions:

Clean the Portobello Mushrooms:
- Wipe the Portobello mushrooms with a damp cloth to remove any dirt. Remove the stems by gently twisting them off or using a spoon to scoop them out.

Prepare the Marinade:
- In a small bowl, whisk together balsamic vinegar, soy sauce or tamari, olive oil, minced garlic, dried thyme, salt, and black pepper to create the marinade.

Marinate the Mushrooms:

- Place the Portobello mushrooms in a shallow dish, gill side up. Pour the marinade over the mushrooms, ensuring they are well coated. Let them marinate for at least 15-30 minutes, flipping them halfway through.

Preheat the Grill or Pan:

- Preheat your grill or a stovetop grill pan over medium-high heat.

Grill the Portobello Mushrooms:

- Place the marinated mushrooms on the grill or pan, gill side down. Grill for about 4-5 minutes per side, or until they are tender and have grill marks.

Toast the Burger Buns (Optional):

- If desired, you can toast the whole grain burger buns on the grill or in a toaster for a minute or two.

Assemble the Burgers:

- Place each grilled Portobello mushroom on a toasted bun. Add your favorite toppings and condiments.

Serve:

- Serve the Portobello mushroom burgers hot with a side of salad, sweet potato fries, or your preferred side dish.

Enjoy:

- Enjoy your flavorful and satisfying Portobello mushroom burgers!

These burgers are not only delicious but also a great source of umami flavor. Feel free to get creative with toppings and condiments to suit your taste. Portobello mushroom burgers are a healthy and hearty option for those looking to enjoy a plant-based meal.

Crockpot/Slow Cooker Meals:

Chicken and Vegetable Stew

Ingredients:

- 1.5 lbs (about 700g) boneless, skinless chicken thighs or breasts, cut into bite-sized pieces
- 2 tablespoons olive oil
- 1 onion, finely chopped
- 3 cloves garlic, minced
- 3 carrots, peeled and sliced
- 2 celery stalks, sliced
- 1 bell pepper, diced
- 1 cup green beans, trimmed and cut into bite-sized pieces
- 1 can (14 oz/400g) diced tomatoes
- 4 cups chicken broth
- 1 teaspoon dried thyme
- 1 teaspoon dried rosemary
- Salt and black pepper, to taste
- 1 cup frozen peas
- 1/4 cup all-purpose flour (optional, for thickening)
- Fresh parsley, chopped, for garnish (optional)

Instructions:

Brown the Chicken:

- Heat olive oil in a large pot over medium-high heat. Add the chicken pieces and brown them on all sides. This step adds flavor to the stew. Once browned, remove the chicken and set it aside.

Sauté Onions and Garlic:

- In the same pot, add chopped onions and garlic. Sauté until the onions are softened and aromatic.

Add Vegetables:

- Add carrots, celery, bell pepper, and green beans to the pot. Cook for a few minutes until the vegetables start to soften.

Combine Chicken and Tomatoes:

- Return the browned chicken to the pot. Add the diced tomatoes with their juice. Stir well to combine.

Pour Chicken Broth:

- Pour in the chicken broth. Add dried thyme, dried rosemary, salt, and black pepper. Bring the mixture to a simmer.

Simmer:

- Reduce the heat to low, cover the pot, and let the stew simmer for about 20-25 minutes until the chicken is cooked through and the vegetables are tender.

Add Peas:

- Add frozen peas to the stew and stir. If you'd like a thicker stew, you can mix 1/4 cup of all-purpose flour with a bit of water to create a slurry and stir it into the stew. Simmer for an additional 5-10 minutes.

Adjust Seasoning:

- Taste the stew and adjust the seasoning with salt and pepper according to your preference.

Serve:

- Ladle the chicken and vegetable stew into bowls. Garnish with chopped fresh parsley if desired.

Enjoy:

- Serve the stew hot and enjoy a comforting and nutritious meal!

Feel free to customize the recipe by adding other vegetables or herbs based on your taste. This chicken and vegetable stew is versatile and perfect for warming up on chilly days.

Lentil and Vegetable Soup

Ingredients:

- 1 cup dry lentils (green or brown), rinsed and drained
- 1 onion, finely chopped
- 2 carrots, peeled and diced
- 2 celery stalks, diced
- 3 cloves garlic, minced
- 1 bell pepper, diced
- 1 can (14 oz/400g) diced tomatoes
- 6 cups vegetable broth
- 1 teaspoon ground cumin
- 1 teaspoon ground coriander
- 1/2 teaspoon smoked paprika
- 1 bay leaf
- Salt and black pepper, to taste
- 2 tablespoons olive oil
- Fresh parsley or cilantro, chopped, for garnish (optional)
- Lemon wedges, for serving (optional)

Instructions:

Prepare Lentils:

- Rinse the lentils under cold water and drain.

Sauté Vegetables:

- In a large pot, heat olive oil over medium heat. Add chopped onion, carrots, celery, garlic, and bell pepper. Sauté for about 5 minutes until the vegetables are softened.

Add Lentils and Spices:

- Add the rinsed lentils to the pot, followed by ground cumin, ground coriander, smoked paprika, bay leaf, salt, and black pepper. Stir well to coat the lentils and vegetables with the spices.

Add Tomatoes and Broth:

- Pour in the diced tomatoes (with their juice) and vegetable broth. Bring the mixture to a boil.

Simmer:

- Reduce the heat to low, cover the pot, and let the soup simmer for about 25-30 minutes or until the lentils are tender.

Adjust Seasoning:

- Taste the soup and adjust the seasoning with salt and pepper if needed. Remove the bay leaf.

Serve:

- Ladle the lentil and vegetable soup into bowls. Garnish with chopped fresh parsley or cilantro if desired.

Serve with Lemon (Optional):

- You can serve the soup with lemon wedges on the side. Squeezing a bit of fresh lemon juice before eating adds a bright and refreshing flavor.

Enjoy:

- Serve the lentil and vegetable soup hot and enjoy a nutritious and comforting meal!

Feel free to customize this recipe by adding other vegetables, such as spinach or kale, or experimenting with different herbs and spices. Lentil and vegetable soup is not only delicious but also a great source of protein and fiber.

Turkey Chili with Lots of Beans and Tomatoes

Ingredients:

- 1 lb ground turkey
- 1 tablespoon olive oil
- 1 large onion, chopped
- 3 cloves garlic, minced
- 1 bell pepper, chopped (any color)
- 2 celery stalks, chopped
- 1 can (14 oz/400g) diced tomatoes
- 2 cans (15 oz each) kidney beans, drained and rinsed
- 1 can (15 oz) black beans, drained and rinsed
- 1 can (15 oz) pinto beans, drained and rinsed
- 1 can (6 oz) tomato paste
- 2 cups chicken or turkey broth
- 2 teaspoons ground cumin
- 2 teaspoons chili powder
- 1 teaspoon dried oregano
- 1 teaspoon smoked paprika
- Salt and black pepper, to taste
- Optional toppings: shredded cheese, chopped green onions, sour cream, avocado slices

Instructions:

    Cook Turkey:

- In a large pot or Dutch oven, heat olive oil over medium heat. Add ground turkey and cook until browned, breaking it apart with a spoon as it cooks.

Sauté Vegetables:
- Add chopped onion, minced garlic, bell pepper, and celery to the pot. Cook for 5-7 minutes until the vegetables are softened.

Add Tomatoes and Beans:
- Stir in diced tomatoes, kidney beans, black beans, pinto beans, and tomato paste.

Pour in Broth:
- Add chicken or turkey broth to the pot. Stir well to combine.

Season the Chili:
- Add ground cumin, chili powder, dried oregano, smoked paprika, salt, and black pepper. Adjust the seasoning according to your taste.

Simmer:
- Bring the chili to a simmer, then reduce the heat to low. Cover and let it simmer for at least 30-40 minutes to allow the flavors to meld. Stir occasionally.

Adjust Consistency:
- If the chili is too thick, you can add more broth until you reach your desired consistency.

Serve:
- Ladle the turkey chili into bowls. Top with shredded cheese, chopped green onions, sour cream, or avocado slices if desired.

Enjoy:
- Serve the turkey chili hot and enjoy a hearty and satisfying meal!

This turkey chili is versatile, and you can adjust the spice level or add additional vegetables based on your preferences. It's perfect for a cozy dinner or for serving at gatherings.

Wraps and Roll-Ups:

Turkey and Avocado Wraps with Whole Wheat Tortillas

Ingredients:

- 4 whole wheat tortillas
- 1 pound sliced turkey breast (smoked or roasted)
- 2 ripe avocados, sliced
- 1 cup cherry tomatoes, halved
- 1/2 red onion, thinly sliced
- 1 cup fresh spinach or arugula leaves
- 1/2 cup Greek yogurt or sour cream
- 2 tablespoons Dijon mustard or your favorite mustard
- Salt and pepper, to taste
- Optional: Squeeze of fresh lime or lemon juice

Instructions:

Prepare Ingredients:

- Lay out the whole wheat tortillas on a clean surface.

Spread Mustard and Yogurt:

- In a small bowl, mix the Dijon mustard with Greek yogurt or sour cream. Spread this mixture evenly on each tortilla.

Layer Turkey Slices:

- Place an even layer of turkey slices on each tortilla, leaving a border around the edges.

Add Avocado Slices:

- Top the turkey with slices of ripe avocado. If you like, you can drizzle a bit of lime or lemon juice over the avocado for added freshness.

Add Vegetables:

- Sprinkle halved cherry tomatoes and thinly sliced red onion over the turkey and avocado.

Add Greens:

- Place a handful of fresh spinach or arugula leaves on top of the other ingredients.

Season with Salt and Pepper:

- Season the wraps with salt and pepper to taste.

Wrap the Ingredients:

- Carefully fold the sides of each tortilla toward the center, and then roll it up tightly from the bottom to form a wrap.

Slice and Serve:

- If desired, slice the wraps in half diagonally for easy serving. Serve immediately.

Enjoy:

- Enjoy your turkey and avocado wraps as a nutritious and satisfying meal!

Feel free to customize the wraps by adding other ingredients such as shredded cheese, sliced cucumber, or your favorite sauce. These wraps are versatile and can be adapted to suit your taste preferences. They are also great for a quick and portable meal on the go.

Veggie Roll-Ups with Hummus

Ingredients:

- Whole wheat or spinach tortillas (large)
- Hummus (store-bought or homemade)
- Assorted fresh vegetables (carrots, cucumbers, bell peppers, cherry tomatoes, etc.), julienned or sliced
- Fresh spinach or lettuce leaves
- Optional: Feta cheese or goat cheese (crumbled)
- Salt and pepper, to taste

Instructions:

Prepare Ingredients:
- Wash and prepare your vegetables by cutting them into thin, julienned strips or slices.

Spread Hummus:
- Lay out a whole wheat or spinach tortilla on a clean surface. Spread a layer of hummus evenly over the entire surface of the tortilla.

Add Vegetables:
- Place a layer of fresh spinach or lettuce leaves over the hummus. Arrange julienned or sliced vegetables on top.

Optional: Add Cheese:
- If you like, sprinkle crumbled feta cheese or goat cheese over the vegetables for added flavor.

Season:

- Season the vegetables with a pinch of salt and pepper to taste.

Roll-Up:
- Starting from one edge, tightly roll the tortilla to form a wrap. Make sure to keep the ingredients compact as you roll.

Slice and Serve:
- Once rolled, use a sharp knife to slice the wrap into smaller roll-up pieces.

Secure with Toothpicks (Optional):
- If serving as an appetizer, you can secure each roll-up with a toothpick to keep it intact.

Arrange and Garnish:
- Arrange the veggie roll-ups on a serving platter. If you have extra vegetables, you can scatter them around the platter for garnish.

Serve:
- Serve the veggie roll-ups immediately as a healthy and delicious snack or appetizer.

These veggie roll-ups are not only visually appealing but also a great way to enjoy a variety of fresh vegetables. You can customize the recipe by adding your favorite vegetables or experimenting with different types of hummus. They are perfect for parties, picnics, or as a quick and nutritious snack.

Smoked Salmon Pinwheels with Low-Fat Cream Cheese

Ingredients:

- 4 large whole wheat or spinach tortillas
- 8 oz (about 227g) low-fat cream cheese, softened
- 8 oz (about 227g) smoked salmon, thinly sliced
- 1 cucumber, thinly sliced
- 1/4 red onion, thinly sliced
- Fresh dill, chopped (for garnish)
- Lemon zest (optional)
- Salt and black pepper, to taste

Instructions:

Prepare Ingredients:
- Lay out the tortillas on a clean surface.

Spread Cream Cheese:
- Spread a layer of softened low-fat cream cheese evenly over the entire surface of each tortilla.

Layer Smoked Salmon:
- Place a layer of smoked salmon slices over the cream cheese, covering the entire surface.

Add Cucumber and Onion:
- Arrange thinly sliced cucumber and red onion over the smoked salmon.

Season and Garnish:

- Sprinkle a pinch of salt and black pepper over the vegetables. Garnish with chopped fresh dill and, if desired, a bit of lemon zest for extra flavor.

Roll-Up:
- Starting from one edge, tightly roll each tortilla to form a log or cylinder. Make sure to keep the ingredients compact as you roll.

Chill:
- Place the rolled-up tortillas in the refrigerator for about 30 minutes to allow them to firm up.

Slice and Serve:
- Once chilled, use a sharp knife to slice the rolled-up tortillas into pinwheels, about 1/2 to 1 inch thick.

Arrange on a Platter:
- Arrange the smoked salmon pinwheels on a serving platter.

Garnish and Serve:
- Garnish with additional fresh dill and lemon zest if desired. Serve the pinwheels immediately.

These smoked salmon pinwheels are not only visually appealing but also a delightful combination of creamy, savory, and fresh flavors. They are perfect for gatherings, brunches, or as an elegant appetizer. Feel free to customize the recipe by adding capers, chives, or other herbs to suit your taste.

Pizza:

Whole Wheat Pizza with Lots of Veggies

Ingredients:

For the Whole Wheat Pizza Dough:

- 2 1/4 teaspoons (1 packet) active dry yeast
- 1 cup warm water (110°F/43°C)
- 1 teaspoon honey or maple syrup
- 2 1/2 cups whole wheat flour
- 1 tablespoon olive oil
- 1 teaspoon salt

For the Pizza Toppings:

- 1/2 cup tomato sauce or pizza sauce
- 1 1/2 cups shredded part-skim mozzarella cheese
- Assorted veggies, thinly sliced or chopped (e.g., bell peppers, cherry tomatoes, red onion, mushrooms, spinach, zucchini)
- 1 tablespoon olive oil
- 1 teaspoon dried oregano
- Salt and black pepper, to taste
- Optional: Red pepper flakes or Parmesan cheese for extra flavor

Instructions:

1. Prepare the Whole Wheat Pizza Dough:

- In a bowl, combine warm water, honey (or maple syrup), and yeast. Let it sit for about 5 minutes, or until the mixture becomes frothy.
- In a large mixing bowl, combine whole wheat flour and salt. Make a well in the center and pour in the yeast mixture and olive oil.
- Mix the ingredients until a dough forms. Knead the dough on a floured surface for about 5-7 minutes until it becomes smooth and elastic.
- Place the dough in a lightly oiled bowl, cover it with a damp cloth, and let it rise in a warm place for about 1 hour or until it doubles in size.

2. Preheat the Oven:

- Preheat your oven to 475°F (245°C). If you have a pizza stone, place it in the oven during the preheating.

3. Roll Out the Dough:

- Punch down the risen dough and divide it into two portions for two pizzas. On a floured surface, roll out each portion into your desired pizza shape and thickness.

4. Assemble the Pizza:

- Transfer the rolled-out dough to a pizza stone or a baking sheet lined with parchment paper.
- Spread a thin layer of tomato sauce over the dough, leaving a small border around the edges.
- Sprinkle shredded mozzarella cheese evenly over the sauce.
- Arrange the sliced or chopped veggies on top of the cheese.

- Drizzle olive oil over the veggies and sprinkle with dried oregano, salt, and black pepper. Add red pepper flakes or Parmesan cheese if desired.

5. Bake:

- Bake the pizza in the preheated oven for 12-15 minutes, or until the crust is golden and the cheese is bubbly and slightly browned.

6. Slice and Serve:

- Remove the pizza from the oven and let it cool for a few minutes. Slice it into wedges or squares, and serve hot.

Enjoy your whole wheat pizza with a variety of colorful and nutritious veggies! Feel free to get creative with the toppings and adjust the quantities based on your preferences.

Chicken and Vegetable Pizza with a Thin Crust

Ingredients:

For the Thin Crust:

- 2 1/4 teaspoons (1 packet) active dry yeast
- 1 cup warm water (110°F/43°C)
- 1 teaspoon sugar
- 2 1/2 cups all-purpose flour
- 1 teaspoon salt
- 2 tablespoons olive oil

For the Pizza Toppings:

- 1/2 cup tomato sauce or pizza sauce
- 1 1/2 cups cooked and shredded chicken breast
- 1 bell pepper, thinly sliced
- 1/2 red onion, thinly sliced
- 1 cup cherry tomatoes, halved
- 1 cup shredded mozzarella cheese
- 1 tablespoon olive oil
- 1 teaspoon dried oregano
- Salt and black pepper, to taste
- Fresh basil or parsley for garnish (optional)

Instructions:

1. Prepare the Thin Crust:

- In a small bowl, combine warm water, sugar, and yeast. Let it sit for about 5 minutes, or until the mixture becomes frothy.
- In a large mixing bowl, combine all-purpose flour and salt. Make a well in the center and pour in the yeast mixture and olive oil.
- Mix the ingredients until a dough forms. Knead the dough on a floured surface for about 5-7 minutes until it becomes smooth and elastic.
- Place the dough in a lightly oiled bowl, cover it with a damp cloth, and let it rest for about 30 minutes.

2. Preheat the Oven:

    - Preheat your oven to the highest temperature it can reach (usually around 475°F/245°C). If you have a pizza stone, place it in the oven during the preheating.

3. Roll Out the Dough:

    - After the dough has rested, roll it out on a floured surface to your desired thinness.
    - If using a pizza stone, transfer the rolled-out dough onto a piece of parchment paper placed on a pizza peel or another baking sheet.

4. Assemble the Pizza:

    - Spread a thin layer of tomato sauce over the rolled-out dough, leaving a small border around the edges.
    - Evenly distribute the shredded chicken, sliced bell pepper, red onion, cherry tomatoes, and mozzarella cheese over the sauce.
    - Drizzle olive oil over the toppings and sprinkle with dried oregano, salt, and black pepper.

5. Bake:

    - If using a pizza stone, carefully transfer the pizza (with parchment paper) onto the preheated stone in the oven.
    - Bake for about 10-12 minutes or until the crust is golden and the cheese is melted and bubbly.

6. Garnish and Serve:

    - Remove the pizza from the oven and let it cool for a few minutes. Garnish with fresh basil or parsley if desired.
    - Slice the pizza and serve hot. Enjoy your delicious chicken and vegetable pizza with a thin crust!

Margherita Pizza with a Light Cheese Topping

Ingredients:

For the Pizza Dough:

- 2 1/4 teaspoons (1 packet) active dry yeast
- 1 cup warm water (110°F/43°C)
- 1 teaspoon sugar
- 3 cups all-purpose flour
- 1 teaspoon salt
- 2 tablespoons olive oil

For the Pizza Toppings:

- 1/2 cup tomato sauce or crushed tomatoes
- 1-2 cloves garlic, minced
- 2-3 ripe tomatoes, thinly sliced
- Fresh mozzarella cheese, sliced or torn into small pieces
- Fresh basil leaves
- Extra-virgin olive oil
- Salt and black pepper, to taste

Instructions:

1. Prepare the Pizza Dough:

- In a small bowl, combine warm water, sugar, and yeast. Let it sit for about 5 minutes, or until the mixture becomes frothy.
- In a large mixing bowl, combine all-purpose flour and salt. Make a well in the center and pour in the yeast mixture and olive oil.
- Mix the ingredients until a dough forms. Knead the dough on a floured surface for about 5-7 minutes until it becomes smooth and elastic.
- Place the dough in a lightly oiled bowl, cover it with a damp cloth, and let it rest for about 1-2 hours or until it doubles in size.

2. Preheat the Oven:

- Preheat your oven to the highest temperature it can reach (usually around 475°F/245°C). If you have a pizza stone, place it in the oven during the preheating.

3. Roll Out the Dough:

- After the dough has risen, roll it out on a floured surface to your desired thickness.
- If using a pizza stone, transfer the rolled-out dough onto a piece of parchment paper placed on a pizza peel or another baking sheet.

4. Assemble the Pizza:

- Spread a thin layer of tomato sauce or crushed tomatoes over the rolled-out dough, leaving a small border around the edges.
- Sprinkle minced garlic evenly over the sauce.
- Arrange the sliced tomatoes over the sauce.
- Place slices or torn pieces of fresh mozzarella evenly over the tomatoes.

5. Bake:

- If using a pizza stone, carefully transfer the pizza (with parchment paper) onto the preheated stone in the oven.
- Bake for about 10-12 minutes or until the crust is golden and the cheese is melted and bubbly.

6. Garnish and Serve:

- Remove the pizza from the oven and let it cool for a few minutes.
- Sprinkle fresh basil leaves over the pizza.
- Drizzle extra-virgin olive oil over the pizza and season with salt and black pepper to taste.
- Slice the pizza and serve hot. Enjoy your light and flavorful Margherita pizza!

Stir-Fries:

Tofu and Broccoli Stir-Fry

Ingredients:

For the Stir-Fry Sauce:

- 1/4 cup soy sauce (or tamari for a gluten-free option)
- 2 tablespoons rice vinegar
- 1 tablespoon hoisin sauce
- 1 tablespoon sesame oil
- 1 tablespoon maple syrup or honey
- 1 teaspoon cornstarch

For the Stir-Fry:

- 1 block extra-firm tofu, pressed and cubed
- 3 cups broccoli florets
- 2 tablespoons vegetable oil (for cooking)
- 3 cloves garlic, minced
- 1 tablespoon fresh ginger, grated
- Sesame seeds for garnish (optional)
- Green onions, chopped, for garnish (optional)
- Cooked brown rice or noodles for serving

Instructions:

1. Prepare the Tofu:

- Press the tofu to remove excess water. You can do this by wrapping the tofu block in a clean kitchen towel, placing it on a plate, and putting a heavy object on top. Let it press for at least 15-30 minutes.
- Once pressed, cut the tofu into cubes.

2. Make the Stir-Fry Sauce:

- In a small bowl, whisk together soy sauce, rice vinegar, hoisin sauce, sesame oil, maple syrup (or honey), and cornstarch. Set aside.

3. Cook the Tofu:

- Heat 1 tablespoon of vegetable oil in a large skillet or wok over medium-high heat.
- Add the tofu cubes to the hot skillet and cook until golden brown on all sides, stirring occasionally. This may take about 8-10 minutes. Once cooked, remove the tofu from the skillet and set it aside.

4. Stir-Fry Broccoli:

- In the same skillet, add another tablespoon of vegetable oil if needed. Add minced garlic and grated ginger. Stir-fry for about 1 minute until fragrant.
- Add broccoli florets to the skillet and stir-fry for an additional 4-5 minutes, or until the broccoli is tender-crisp.

5. Combine Tofu and Broccoli:

- Return the cooked tofu to the skillet with the broccoli.
- Pour the stir-fry sauce over the tofu and broccoli. Toss everything together to coat evenly. Cook for an additional 2-3 minutes until the sauce thickens.

6. Serve:

- Serve the tofu and broccoli stir-fry over cooked brown rice or noodles.
- Garnish with sesame seeds and chopped green onions if desired.

7. Enjoy:

- Enjoy your delicious and nutritious tofu and broccoli stir-fry!

Feel free to customize this recipe by adding other vegetables like bell peppers, carrots, or snap peas. Adjust the level of spiciness by adding red pepper flakes or Sriracha if you like it hot.

Shrimp and Snow Pea Stir-Fry

Ingredients:

For the Marinade:

- 1 pound (450g) large shrimp, peeled and deveined
- 2 tablespoons soy sauce
- 1 tablespoon rice vinegar
- 1 tablespoon sesame oil
- 1 teaspoon honey
- 2 cloves garlic, minced
- 1 teaspoon fresh ginger, grated
- 1 tablespoon cornstarch

For the Stir-Fry:

- 2 tablespoons vegetable oil
- 1 pound (450g) snow peas, trimmed
- 1 red bell pepper, thinly sliced
- 3 green onions, sliced
- Cooked rice or noodles for serving

Instructions:

1. Marinate the Shrimp:

- In a bowl, combine soy sauce, rice vinegar, sesame oil, honey, minced garlic, grated ginger, and cornstarch. Stir well to make the marinade.

- Add the peeled and deveined shrimp to the marinade, ensuring they are well-coated. Let them marinate for at least 15-30 minutes.

2. Cook the Snow Peas:

- Heat 1 tablespoon of vegetable oil in a wok or large skillet over medium-high heat.
- Add the trimmed snow peas and stir-fry for about 2-3 minutes until they are bright green and slightly tender. Remove them from the wok and set aside.

3. Cook the Shrimp:

- In the same wok, add another tablespoon of vegetable oil.
- Add the marinated shrimp to the wok and stir-fry for 2-3 minutes or until they turn pink and opaque.
- Remove the shrimp from the wok and set them aside.

4. Stir-Fry Vegetables:

- In the same wok, add sliced red bell pepper and green onions. Stir-fry for 2-3 minutes until the vegetables are slightly tender but still crisp.

5. Combine Ingredients:

- Return the cooked snow peas and shrimp to the wok with the stir-fried vegetables.
- Toss everything together and cook for an additional 1-2 minutes until everything is heated through.

6. Serve:

- Serve the shrimp and snow pea stir-fry over cooked rice or noodles.

7. Enjoy:

- Enjoy your delicious shrimp and snow pea stir-fry!

Feel free to customize this recipe by adding other vegetables like sliced carrots or broccoli. You can also adjust the level of sweetness or spiciness according to your taste preferences.

Chicken and Asparagus Stir-Fry

Ingredients:

For the Marinade:

- 1 pound (about 450g) boneless, skinless chicken breasts, thinly sliced
- 2 tablespoons soy sauce
- 1 tablespoon rice vinegar
- 1 tablespoon hoisin sauce
- 1 tablespoon cornstarch
- 1 teaspoon sesame oil
- 1 teaspoon grated fresh ginger
- 2 cloves garlic, minced

For the Stir-Fry:

- 2 tablespoons vegetable oil
- 1 bunch asparagus, trimmed and cut into bite-sized pieces
- 1 red bell pepper, thinly sliced
- 1 yellow bell pepper, thinly sliced
- 3 green onions, sliced
- Sesame seeds for garnish (optional)
- Cooked rice or noodles for serving

Instructions:

1. Marinate the Chicken:

- In a bowl, combine soy sauce, rice vinegar, hoisin sauce, cornstarch, sesame oil, grated ginger, and minced garlic. Stir well to create the marinade.
- Add the sliced chicken to the marinade, making sure the chicken is well-coated. Allow it to marinate for at least 15-30 minutes.

2. Cook the Asparagus:

- Heat 1 tablespoon of vegetable oil in a wok or large skillet over medium-high heat.
- Add the asparagus pieces and stir-fry for about 2-3 minutes until they are bright green and slightly tender. Remove them from the wok and set aside.

3. Cook the Chicken:

- In the same wok, add another tablespoon of vegetable oil.
- Add the marinated chicken to the wok and stir-fry for 4-5 minutes or until the chicken is cooked through and browned.
- Remove the chicken from the wok and set it aside.

4. Stir-Fry Vegetables:

- In the same wok, add sliced red bell pepper, yellow bell pepper, and green onions. Stir-fry for 2-3 minutes until the vegetables are slightly tender but still crisp.

5. Combine Ingredients:

- Return the cooked asparagus and chicken to the wok with the stir-fried vegetables.

- Toss everything together and cook for an additional 1-2 minutes until everything is heated through.

6. Serve:

- Serve the chicken and asparagus stir-fry over cooked rice or noodles.

7. Garnish and Enjoy:

- Garnish with sesame seeds if desired and enjoy your delicious chicken and asparagus stir-fry!

Feel free to adjust the vegetables or add other favorites like broccoli or snap peas. Customize the level of spiciness by adding red pepper flakes or Sriracha according to your taste preferences.

Sauces and Dressings:

Yogurt-Based Tzatziki Sauce

Ingredients:

- 1 cucumber, finely grated
- 2 cups Greek yogurt (full-fat or low-fat)
- 2 cloves garlic, minced
- 1 tablespoon extra-virgin olive oil
- 1 tablespoon fresh lemon juice
- 1 tablespoon chopped fresh dill
- Salt and pepper, to taste

Instructions:

Prepare the Cucumber:

- Peel the cucumber and grate it using a fine grater. Place the grated cucumber in a clean kitchen towel or cheesecloth and squeeze out excess moisture.

Mix Yogurt and Cucumber:

- In a bowl, combine the Greek yogurt and grated cucumber.

Add Garlic:

- Add the minced garlic to the yogurt and cucumber mixture.

Add Olive Oil:

- Drizzle extra-virgin olive oil over the mixture.

Add Lemon Juice:

- Squeeze fresh lemon juice into the bowl.

Add Fresh Dill:

- Add chopped fresh dill to the mixture. If you don't have fresh dill, you can use dried dill, but fresh dill provides a more vibrant flavor.

Season with Salt and Pepper:

- Season the tzatziki sauce with salt and pepper to taste. Start with a pinch of salt and adjust according to your preference.

Mix Well:

- Mix all the ingredients together until well combined.

Refrigerate:

- Cover the bowl and refrigerate the tzatziki sauce for at least 1-2 hours before serving. This allows the flavors to meld.

Adjust Consistency (Optional):

- If you prefer a thinner consistency, you can add a small amount of water or more lemon juice until you reach your desired thickness.

Serve:

- Serve the tzatziki sauce chilled. It's a perfect accompaniment to various dishes or as a refreshing dip.

Enjoy:

- Enjoy your homemade yogurt-based tzatziki sauce!

Feel free to customize this recipe by adding mint, parsley, or a pinch of cayenne pepper for extra flavor. Adjust the garlic and lemon juice to suit your taste preferences.

Balsamic Vinaigrette with Dijon Mustard

Ingredients:

- 1/3 cup balsamic vinegar
- 1 tablespoon Dijon mustard
- 1 clove garlic, minced (optional)
- 1 teaspoon honey or maple syrup (optional, for sweetness)
- 2/3 cup extra-virgin olive oil
- Salt and black pepper, to taste

Instructions:

Combine Vinegar and Mustard:
- In a bowl or a jar with a tight-fitting lid, combine balsamic vinegar and Dijon mustard.

Add Garlic (Optional):
- If you like a bit of garlic flavor, add minced garlic to the vinegar and mustard mixture.

Add Sweetener (Optional):
- If you prefer a hint of sweetness, you can add honey or maple syrup to the mixture. Adjust the amount based on your taste.

Whisk or Shake:
- Whisk the ingredients together or cover the jar and shake it vigorously to combine.

Slowly Add Olive Oil:

- While continuing to whisk or shake, slowly drizzle in the extra-virgin olive oil. This helps emulsify the dressing.

Season with Salt and Pepper:

- Season the vinaigrette with salt and black pepper to taste. Start with a pinch of salt and adjust as needed.

Taste and Adjust:

- Taste the dressing and adjust the balance of flavors. Add more mustard, honey, or vinegar if necessary.

Store:

- If not using immediately, store the balsamic vinaigrette in a sealed container in the refrigerator. Before using, let it come to room temperature and give it a good shake or whisk.

Serve:

- Use the balsamic vinaigrette to dress your favorite salads, vegetables, or grilled meats.

Enjoy:

- Enjoy the tangy and flavorful balsamic vinaigrette with Dijon mustard on your favorite dishes!

This homemade dressing allows you to control the ingredients and customize the flavor to your liking. Feel free to experiment with the ratios and add herbs like thyme, basil, or oregano for additional depth of flavor.

Salsa Verde with Fresh Herbs

Ingredients:

- 1 cup fresh cilantro leaves, chopped
- 1/2 cup fresh parsley leaves, chopped
- 2 tablespoons fresh mint leaves, chopped
- 1/2 cup fresh green onions (scallions), chopped
- 2 cloves garlic, minced
- 1 jalapeño or serrano pepper, seeds and membranes removed (for milder salsa, use less or omit)
- 2 tablespoons capers, drained
- 2 tablespoons Dijon mustard
- 1 tablespoon honey or agave syrup
- 1/3 cup red wine vinegar
- 2/3 cup extra-virgin olive oil
- Salt and black pepper, to taste

Instructions:

Prepare Fresh Herbs:
- Wash and chop the fresh cilantro, parsley, mint, and green onions.

Prepare Pepper:
- If using a jalapeño or serrano pepper, remove the seeds and membranes for less heat. Wear gloves or wash your hands thoroughly after handling hot peppers.

Combine Ingredients:
- In a food processor or blender, combine the chopped cilantro, parsley, mint, green onions, minced garlic, deseeded pepper, capers, Dijon mustard, honey, and red wine vinegar.

Blend:
- Pulse the ingredients a few times to start breaking them down.

Slowly Add Olive Oil:
- With the processor or blender running, slowly drizzle in the extra-virgin olive oil until the mixture becomes smooth and well combined. Stop and scrape down the sides if needed.

Season:
- Season the salsa verde with salt and black pepper to taste. Adjust the seasoning as necessary.

Taste and Adjust:
- Taste the salsa verde and adjust the balance of flavors. Add more honey, vinegar, or herbs if desired.

Store:
- Transfer the salsa verde to a sealed container or jar. Refrigerate for at least 1 hour to allow the flavors to meld.

Serve:
- Serve the salsa verde as a condiment for grilled meats, seafood, vegetables, or as a dip for tortilla chips.

Enjoy:
- Enjoy the fresh and herby goodness of homemade salsa verde!

This versatile salsa verde can add a burst of flavor to a variety of dishes. Feel free to customize it by adjusting the herbs, heat level, or other ingredients to suit your taste preferences.